You Can Do This

—Intentional Parenting Strategies—

You Can Do This

The Parent's Guide to Grow Love,
Confidence, Happiness, Integrity, and
Resilience in Our Children

Lahna Rung Roche

Cover Art by
Michael I Rung

Published by
MARIALEXANDER
Broussard, Louisiana

ISBN: 978-0-578-70265-0

Dedications

For Liam and Isla – My purpose,
You inspire me to be a better person.

For Collus – My rock,
You support me no matter what as we brave life together.

For Mom & Dad – My basis,
You show me that parenting never ends; it just changes.

Table of Contents

Acknowledgements

I sincerely appreciate the love and support from numerous people in my life that encourage me to share my thoughts with the world. As a private person, sharing this book is both frightening and liberating.

I want to thank my family, all of which have heavily influenced the creation of this book: Collus, for the constant support and strength; Liam and Isla, for the unbridled trust and assistance; Rexine and Jimmy, for the strong foundation and guidance; Jade, Michael and their families, for the shared appreciation and solidarity; and Kelli and Aimée, for the fierce belief and encouragement.

I also want to sincerely thank my voluntary editors, Kelli and Rexine, for providing critical feedback and support during the writing process, including Kelli's kindness for writing the touching foreword, and my artist and publishing guide, Michael, for your creativity and insights.

Additionally, I'd like to thank those who have allowed me to participate in their parenting processes or shared intimate stories and opinions from their parenting experiences, including but not limited to those aforementioned and Annette, Kayla, Debbie, Lisa, Pam, Nanette, and Melissa.

Lastly, I'd like to thank each and every person who takes the time to read and consider the thoughts included in this book. Thank you for your interest and/or commitment to advocate for positive ways to shape the next generation. I believe that our children are the answer to making the world a better place.

Foreword

Like many of you, I answer to several names in my life. My sweet southern family calls me by my full given name, Kelli Robin. My high school friends call me Diet (pronounced Deet), but that is a story for another day. For nearly twenty years of my professional career, I had the privilege and responsibility of facilitating a smooth transition for incoming freshmen at Louisiana State University as well as advising and mentoring a phenomenal group of students called the LSU Ambassadors. My students at LSU affectionately called me K-Webb or K-Dub. However, the sweetest name I answer to, the one I am most fond of, the title that is arguably the most important, challenging, and satisfying of my life is Mom. It seems funny to me now, because the day we brought my son, Parish, home from the hospital, we sat his infant carrier down in the middle of the kitchen, looked at each other and said, "So, what do we do with him now?"

I met Lahna briefly when we were in graduate school together at LSU. She was the type of person people instantly gravitated to. A sweet soul that I could immediately sense was just...good. Someone I genuinely wanted to emulate. Somehow I knew even then that she would be an impactful person in my life. She definitely made a lasting impression on me. A few years later, I had the opportunity to work with Lahna as a colleague on the LSU campus, and we began to forge the kind of deep connection and friendship everyone hopes for in their lives. She was everything I sensed she was, and so much more.

During our professional careers, I watched as Lahna impacted the lives of hundreds of students at LSU. She worked at places on campus such as the University College Center for Freshman Year and the Center for Academic Success. Lahna's passion was teaching students how to learn, how to succeed in college, how to develop strategies they could carry with them that would continue to serve them throughout their lifetimes. She was the best at her job; a truly impactful professional. I was in awe of her patience, her talent for teaching her art, and her genuine desire to see other thrive.

As our friendship flourished, I learned something else about Lahna. She is absolutely the wisest person I know. My friend Aimée and I call her "The Owl". She is insightful. Yet, it's more than that. She encourages and supports those around her to reflect on their experiences so *they* learn how to be insightful themselves. And this is the type of premise she brings to this book. In You Can Do This, Lahna doesn't *tell* us exactly how to grow love, confidence, happiness, integrity and resilience in our children, she *teaches* us techniques and principles. She supports and encourages us as we explore our own values and reflect to develop unique intentional messages tailored to our own families. Then, she guides us on how to implement these strategies by tying it all together and offering real examples taken from her own experience.

Lahna asked me to help edit her book not because I am an expert, but because I am a parent. I agreed to help edit her book because I have seen how she practices these principles with her own children, and I believe in her techniques. I have seen her implement these strategies in her own life, and I have witnessed how successful her efforts have been. The most impactful piece of this book for me is that Lahna focuses on communication between parents and children. She teaches us that, even though they are young, children can understand important concepts, and that our children will rise to the level we expect of them. She guides us on how to hold honest, transparent, intentional and impactful conversations with our children that will stay with them and develop them into the adults we hope in our hearts they will become. Adults who not only contribute to society, but who contribute positively to the lives of others. These techniques are surprisingly easily executed. So much so, that they simply become a way of life, not strategies we have to work to implement.

Lahna put her heart and soul into this book in hopes that sharing her knowledge of learning and development as well as her experience would be impactful for other families. She wants us all to succeed as parents and for our children to truly thrive. We are raising the next generation. With our guidance, they can make this world a better place.

"So, what do we do with him now?" I'm going to follow my dear friend Lahna's lead…and be an intentional parent. I hope you will join me.

Kelli Stevens Webber

About Kelli

Kelli Stevens Webber has been working in higher education for over twenty years in the areas of orientation & transition programs and student records. A true Louisianan, she bleeds purple and gold on Saturdays and black and gold on Sundays. She holds family and friends very dear to her heart; however, the true love of her life is her son, Parish. Born with Down syndrome and full of life lessons, Kelli learns from Parish daily as he models for others how to overcome adversities with a positive attitude and enjoy life to the fullest.

Introduction

Magic wand, easy button, crystal ball; not when it comes to parenting. Unfortunately, there are no magical solutions for parents. We parent each day the best we can with the information we have, without assurances of the outcome. We evaluate numerous options in order to make countless, daily decisions, most of which are not easy. We question each one, analyzing if we are doing things right, and wonder how we are affecting our children, now and later. We wonder who our children will become when we are no longer making the decisions – when they are responsible for their own lives. Will they be independent, successful, healthy, happy? Will they believe in themselves enough to live free from self-inflicted anxiety? Will they be able to cope with life's challenges? Will they develop quality relationships that will sustain them and surround them with love? Will they contribute to the betterment of others? In the end, will they truly be happy with who they are and what they've become? Will we?

In 1943, Maslow authored, "A theory of human motivation", providing a "hierarchy of needs" that gave us a framework to meet the needs of children so that they would become successful adults and avoid mental illness. Since then, it is readily acknowledged that

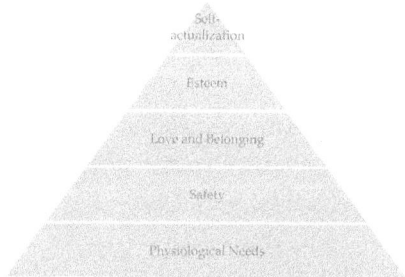

Figure 1. Maslow's Hierarchy of Needs

children need food, water, clothing, sleep, and shelter to survive; love, security, and support to thrive; and confidence, respect, purpose, and morality to reach their fullest potential (Maslow, 1943). As new parents, we anticipate the need to provide children with the necessities to meet their physiological needs (food, water, clothing, sleep, and shelter), to keep them safe, and to love them. Yet, we don't necessarily know how to shape the more complex areas of ensuring that they feel secure and connected, or helping them to develop self-esteem and morality – those necessities that help them thrive and succeed.

How do we help our children develop in the more complex areas? The answer lies in communication. Communication is the basis for helping children learn and grow. Consider why there are so many whys. Children ask copious *why* questions because they don't know the answers but more importantly, they *want* to know. Using their inherent desire to learn is a powerful tool which allows us to age-appropriately inform children about life. As educators of life, parents can use this opportunity early on, not only to provide children with the answers they seek, but to go beyond that by providing them with foundational messages that are motivational and empowering so they may gain much more than mere information. This is an opportunity to be our child's champion – their chief supporter.

Communicating messages to children begins when parenting begins. When we snuggle our crying babies and whisper reassurances, they receive a message of security and safety. When we kiss our toddler's bumps and bruises and promise it will get better, they receive a message that this ailment is temporary and they will endure it. Our messages are powerful and lasting. Why not use them intentionally? Because, when we think them through and create messages that are deliberate, our intent (what we hope will occur) and the impact (what actually does) has a greater chance of being one and the same.

As a parent, I want to teach my children lessons that will not only make them successful, but make them great people who love, are kind, have self-confidence, and are resilient as they face life's challenges. As a mental health professional, I want them to make good choices, have healthy beliefs about themselves, respect others, and develop coping strategies to manage life. And, as an educator, I believe that through the messages we tell our children, they understand our expectations and priorities and use them as the foundation of how they see and interact with themselves and the world around them.

Consistent messaging can help to set expectations and priorities for young children. The more they hear regular and consistent messages, the more likely they are to embrace them, understand them, believe them, and use them. For example, there are two simple rules my children must follow, particularly when I am not with them: *Behave* and *Have Fun*. This was their very first lesson and has reigned supreme in our rule category thus far. Upon introduction, I gave them a simple explanation of what behave means and the expectations associated it. I also explained my hope that they enjoy life by finding the fun in their experiences. Additionally, I pointed out that if they are not behaving, no one is having fun because their behavior not only impacts themselves, but it impacts others. I no longer give the full explanation. I simply ask, "What are my two rules?" and they bellow back, "Behave and have fun!" Those two simple rules embody what I want for them as they live through childhood. I want them to listen, respect others, make good choices (behave), and enjoy new experiences by choosing to participate and recognize the joy in things (have fun).

2 RULES
- Behave
- Have Fun

In addition to the two rules, I have spewed many messages over the years; some simple and some more complex, but all deliberate in purpose, intentional – to empower my children into believing in themselves and being the best they can be. Over time, I hope these messages become the foundation of their self-talk – *the way in which they talk to themselves*. Because when we talk to ourselves in positive, realistic ways (positive self-talk), we lead healthier, happier lives. Conversely, when we talk to ourselves in negative ways (negative self-talk), we engage in a self-destructive habit which may result in undue anxiety and depression.

The information contained in this book is based off of my personal practices with my own children. The messages were developed based on my training and experiences in psychology, mental health counseling, and education, and combine research, theory, and practice with my personal observations and applications as a parent. Since much of the information shared throughout this book is based on my own values, beliefs, opinions, and practices, parents should evaluate the contents to determine if the information is applicable to them and their children.

The purpose of this book is to provide parents and caregivers with a new parenting strategy, intentional messaging, to shape children into becoming the greatest version of themselves by using systematic messaging. It is not meant to be comprehensive or restrictive, but to allow parents an opportunity to identify expectations and priorities to meet the needs of their children and family, which may lead to the creation of better messages, personalized for their child. It is meant to teach children how to talk to themselves in positive and realistic ways. And, it is meant to facilitate active dialogue and discussion with them in order to establish strong parent-child relationships leading into adolescence. It is a way for parents to give their children a gift – messages they can bring with them into adulthood.

The messages shared are categorized into five areas: love, confidence, happiness, integrity, and resilience. Each message includes:

> An *exploration* section containing explanations regarding the intent behind the message and how it benefits our children;

> An *implementation* section containing recommendations for when and how to use the message, including example scenarios;

> An *evaluation* section containing personal parent and child perspectives on the use of the message; and

> A *reflection* section containing questions to consider in order to determine if you will adopt the message or develop your own.

When used initially, these messages should be accompanied by an age-appropriate explanation as to why it applies to a particular situation and expectations for the future. It should encourage discussion in which we allow our child to ask questions to clarify our intent and/or ask our child questions to ensure understanding. Through discussions, even very young children learn to understand larger concepts and rise to the expectations we set for them. After repeated use, these messages become a reminder in other relevant situations which may not require an entire explanation or lecture. It is also important to note that our actions must match our words in order for the messages to be genuine and for our children to believe us.

My hope is that by sharing these messages, other parents will find this parenting strategy useful in identifying their values, expectations, and priorities and use messaging as a way to inspire children into being the best they can be so that they may lead healthy and happy lives. And, that by hearing these messages, children will thrive and succeed by being empowered to embrace love, believe their worth, choose happiness, be honest, and brave life.

Part 1 ~ Love

Intentional Messages That Nurture Love

Intentional Messages That Nurture Love

Love – an intense feeling of deep affection (Oxford Living Dictionaries)

What is parental love?

Parents know what love feels like, whether they've experienced it once or a number of times. Parental love is *a deep affection for our children*. It can happen in an instance; when we discover we are expecting a child; when we adopt a child; when we meet our child. It can also happen over time, as love tends to grow and develop as our relationship with our child grows and develops. Regardless of the setting, the time, or the circumstances, we typically experience feelings of affection, commitment, and/or wonder, when we recognize our love for our child.

As new parents, we make promises to our children. We promise to protect them, be the best parent we can be, and to love them forever. Then, we may have wondered, what do I do now? Because becoming a parent, no matter how, requires a very real responsibility to be someone our children can depend on, each and every day, forever. They look to us for everything – knowledge, guidance, protection, encouragement, and love. As parents, the love we give our children must be true, unwavering, and everlasting, without fail.

How do I nurture love in my children?

Raising children in an environment of love is the foundation for giving them a happy childhood. Actions are important; cuddles, hugs, following through on our promises, all demonstrate our love. Still, saying the words "I love you" is an easy place to begin, particularly with young children. They believe in us and in everything that we say.

"I love you" is a clear statement essential for them to rely upon should any doubt arise as they age.

Why nurture love using intentional messaging?

Nurturing love through messaging encourages children to be loving themselves. It sets them up to create an inner-being that begins in love, which in turn fosters more positive thoughts, emotions and behaviors, all of which promote health and happiness. It encourages them to function from a place of goodness, free from worry, fear, hate, or anger. Love can be misinterpreted as a weakness, but in reality when children grow in love, they are happy and possess the strength and courage to try new things, spread their wings, and face life's challenge. Finally, teaching children about love provides them with a foundation to love as adults, with significant others, friends, and their own children.

Let's explore the messages that nurture love and belonging in our children.

Chapter 1
Unconditional Love

I love you no matter what!

What is the message?

I love you no matter what!

What is the purpose of the message?

The purpose of the message, I love you no matter what, is to demonstrate unconditional love.

EXPLORATION

What is unconditional love in the parent-child relationship?

Adding the phrase "no matter what" to "I love you", promotes a love that is exceedingly valuable – unconditional love – *love free from conditions or limits*. Unconditional love is easily recognized when a child is born (Welwood, 1985) because when we become parents, we experience love that is unabashed, intense, and profound. And, we vividly recognize what it means to love our children without limits. We also benefit from the reciprocation of unconditional love. Yes, our children love and accept us wholeheartedly and unconditionally. As they place their unbridled trust and love in us, we have a responsibility to do the same with them. For some new parents, their own first experience with unconditional love occurs when they become parents themselves.

Why nurture love that is unconditional with my children?

Continuing to provide children with unwavering love facilitates healthy development (Maslow, 1943). As young children navigate learning how to make good choices and behave, it is important to provide them with reassurances and reminders that our love is constant. This permits them to make mistakes which encourages them to experience life. When children feel secure in how we feel for them, they have the courage to try new things, explore, develop, and learn, free from worry about our feelings for them. Furthermore, by modeling unconditional love with our children, we are also affecting the next generation. Our children are more likely to provide their children (our grandchildren) with unconditional love because we become their primary, educational source of how they will parent.

Why is it important to reaffirm that my love is unconditional?

Most parents will assert that they love their children without limits. But, do our children understand and believe this to be true? For the young mind, understanding that our love is permanent is a difficult task, particularly when they are corrected and little ones are corrected often. Think of how many times we tell a 3-year-old "no" each day. Each time they are corrected for an unfavorable behavior, they wonder if we still love them. This may cause feelings of discomfort, sadness, or anxiety; sometimes the negative feelings they are experiencing are due to their fear of losing our love, not their original misstep. After correcting a behavior and setting expectations for the future, it is important to provide reassurances to reaffirm that we love them without fail.

If I love my children no matter what, am I encouraging them to do bad things?

Loving unconditionally does not encourage children to do bad things because they know that we will love them anyway. Their security in the knowledge that our love is constant, does the opposite; it encourages them do their best to meet the expectations we set for them. Most times, it encourages them to behave because they are not seeking our attention through misbehavior. It also allows them to develop as individuals, distinct from us in personality, interests, preferences, and temperament. And, it gives us an opportunity to recognize them for being that individual, separate from us.

There will be many instances where we do not condone our child's choices, attitudes, or actions. Loving unconditionally does not free us from teaching or guiding our children. We must teach them how to act in the world, introduce them to new experiences, and correct their behaviors. Yet, we do so in such a way that lets everyone move past a mishap and reaffirms that our love is constant. Our love is not conditional on those choices, attitudes, or actions.

IMPLEMENTATION

When do I tell my children, I love you no matter what?

This message may be used on a regular, ongoing basis, in a multitude of situations, and under many circumstances, including triumphs, failures, and everyday life. Repeating the message is important for children to accept the statement as truth, believing that we love them no matter the situation or circumstance, for the long haul, without limits or conditions. This is clearly important for very young children but never stops being a comforting and necessary message for all children.

How do I use the message – I love you no matter what?

Because this message can be used on a regular basis and for many situations, it is relatively easy to tell our children we love them no matter what – when they wake up, when we part ways for the day, when they go to bed. It is also a good way to end a discussion, especially one where we need to address a mishap. During these discussions, it is helpful to gain insight into a child's motivation for their misbehavior. Therefore, asking questions to facilitate discussion allows us to better help them deal with the root cause of their choices in order for us to teach them how to behave in the future. It also gives them an opportunity to contemplate their choices, identify their emotions, and come up with other, more appropriate responses to their situation.

The following example uses this message after a young child makes a mistake. Note that very young children give very simple, often one-word, answers. As they age and develop, the dialogue will increase. Yet, we are setting the framework for the parent-child interaction during these situations by asking questions and facilitating dialogue when our children are young.

Example Scenario

Example situation.
3 year old hits another child.

Example reaction-interaction.
Parent: Let's talk about what happened. Tell me why you hit them.
Child: They took my blocks.
Parent: How did you feel when they took your blocks?
Child: Mad.
Parent: I understand that when they took your blocks you felt mad. We all get angry sometimes. But, we do not hit others even when we are mad. It is not acceptable behavior because we could really hurt someone. It is never okay to use our hands to hurt other people. What could you have done instead of hitting them?
Child: Tell them to give the blocks back.
Parent: Yes, or you could ask them if they want to play with the blocks with you. Which do you prefer?
Child: Asking them to play.
Parent: Good, now you have two options next time someone takes your blocks. You can ask them to give them back or ask them to play with you. But, you will not hit them.
Child: Okay.
Parent: You are learning how to act with your friends. Now you know it is never okay to hit others. I expect you to apologize to them for hitting them.
Child: Okay.
Parent: What will you say to them when you apologize?
Child: I'm sorry for hitting you.
Parent: Okay. Now, tell me how you feel about getting in trouble.
Child: Sad.
Parent: You will make mistakes. I'm going to teach you how to make better choices and you will learn. I want you to know that *I*

love you no matter what. This did not change my love for you. Do you understand?
Child: Yes.

There are numerous approaches we could take when responding to the above example. Yet, although simplified, this example follows the method of addressing the behavior, exploring the root cause of the choice, providing other options for handling the situation, and setting expectations for future situations. Most essentially, it demonstrates how to reassure our child that our love has not changed based on their poor choice. Using intentional messaging reinforces that our love is unconditional.

EVALUATION

As a parent, why do I use this message?

When I tell my children that I love them no matter what, I hope they truly believe that my love is intense, powerful, meaningful, everlasting, and without any conditions on who they are now, who they will become, and how they behave. I want them to feel the care I have for them, understand that it is permanent, and know that they do not need to work to gain my love. My love is *free* and flowing for them. And, it always will be.

As a child, what does this message mean to me and how does it make me feel?

I feel happy. It means a lot to me because it means you know me really good and you love me even if I do bad things. No matter what I do, no matter where I am, you love me.

REFLECTION

What do I think about this message?

Take a moment to reflect on using the message, *I love you no matter what.* Ask yourself:

> ➤ Does it match the way I feel about my children?
> ➤ Does it help to build our parent-child relationship?
> ➤ Am I comfortable saying it out loud?
> ➤ Does it reflect a message that I want my children to understand and believe?
> ➤ Does it help me to encourage my children to be happy?
> ➤ Does it help me to alleviate my children's feelings of anxiety or sadness?

What intentional message will I use?

Based on your reflection, consider whether to adopt this message or to modify it for your use. If you chose something different, create your own message by writing it here.

I will nurture unconditional love in my children by saying ...

Chapter 2
Comfort

I'm giving you my love, do you feel it?

What is the message?

I'm giving you my love, do you feel it?

What is the purpose of the message?

The purpose of the message, I'm giving you my love, do you feel it, is to provide comfort to our children.

EXPLORATION

What does it mean to provide comfort to my children?

When we provide comfort to our children, we seek to *alleviate distress* they are experiencing. We readily comfort our infants and toddlers. We provide comfort to our crying newborns by picking them up, rocking them, or soothing them. We provide comfort to our newly-mobile toddlers when they get bumps or bruises by holding them, tending to their injury, reassuring them, and encouraging them to try again. We are also quick to comfort our children during serious situations such as when they are facing illnesses or after the death of a loved one. Furthermore, research confirms that parent comforting helps children during medical procedures (Bauchner et al., 1994). Providing comfort for our children equates to showing them care and compassion in their times of need.

Why is it important for my children to feel comforted?

The importance of comfort is evident early on in a child's life but is equally important in young childhood and for situations that may not be quite as severe as death or illness yet still provoke negative feelings and reactions. Comforting children when they are sad, scared, or uneasy, reduces their anxiety, a root cause of many childhood misconducts. If anxiety remains persistent in young children it can potentially produce a mental illness diagnosis later in life.

Through comfort, children also gain a strategy to combat negative feelings. That strategy is to ask for and accept help and love from others without shame or embarrassment. It encourages them to trust us, gain strength from the relationships they build, and use the love they receive from us endure life.

How does comforting my children benefit the parent-child relationship?

Providing comfort to our children reinforces our love. It demonstrates to them that they can trust us to be present, especially when they need us. Our comfort encourages them to share their feelings with us. It strengthens the parent-child relationship by creating a compassionate relationship, encouraging our children to let us into their world. And, it lessens feelings of loneliness by confirming to them that they are not alone in this world. We are with them in this journey. This sense of togetherness will be incredibly valuable for them (and for us) in their adolescent years.

If I give my children comfort, will I make them dependent?

Comforting our children during their stressful times, does not make them weak or dependent on us. It conveys a sense of humanity, reinforces our love for them, and lessens their fears over stressful situations. It gives them encouragement to face life's challenges or provides a sense of relief after difficult situations, all reinforcing a relationship built on love, understanding, and compassion.

Providing comfort should not be confused with eliminating all obstacles, which can cause dependence. We do not remove all possible causes of distress, as encountering stressful situations is a natural part of experiencing life and would be counter-productive to encouraging independence. We merely respond to the stressful situations by showing compassion and care in order to help reduce fears or sadness and provide relief for our children.

IMPLEMENTATION

When do I tell my children, I'm giving you my love, do you feel it?

This message may be used in a multitude of situations, but is most effective in attempting to alleviate distress and therefore, should be used in those instances when our children need that extra bit of love and support. It is particularly helpful when they are facing something sad, anxiety-provoking, overwhelming, or down-right scary. Example situations include after the death of a pet (sad), before their very first graded test (anxiety-provoking), after they've attempted and failed to ride their bike (overwhelming), or when they have to have surgery (down-right scary).

How do I use the message – I'm giving you my love, do you feel it?

This message is best used with a physical gesture (a big hug, a blown kiss) that shows us giving our love to them. Saying that I'm giving you my love, do you feel it, is a way for our children to mindfully acknowledge and accept our love in that particular situation. It is a good way to end a discussion on whatever stress they are experiencing in order for them to gain the courage to encounter the situation or as a comfort for something sad or scary that may have already occurred.

The following, brief example uses this message during a down-right scary situation for both the parents and the children.

Example Scenario

Example situation.
5 year old child needs minor surgery.

Example reaction-interaction.
Parent: How are you feeling about this procedure?
Child: Scared.
Parent: Tell me about your fears.
Child: I don't know what they will do and that scares me.
Parent: Let's talk about the procedure. They will give you medicine, put you to sleep, and fix the problem. When they are finished, we will meet you in recovery. Do you have any questions?
Child: Yes. Will it hurt?

Parent: It will probably hurt some but they will give you medicine so that it doesn't hurt during the procedure. If it hurts after, they can give you medicine for that, too. You can tell me if it hurts then.
Child: Okay. I'll tell you if it hurts. I'm still scared.
Parent: I understand that this is scary because it is a new experience and you may have some pain. We must do it to fix this problem so that you can be healthy. And, I'm going to give you all my strength and love to help you through. How about a hug?
Child: Okay.
(Heart-to heart connection hug)
Parent: I'm giving you my love. Do you feel it?
Child: Yes.

With children, honesty is extremely important so that they fully trust us and our words. Therefore, any time a child is going through a medical procedure, it is important to let them know that there will be pain, if it will in fact be painful. It is also important to provide age-appropriate information with minimum details as not to amplify their fears over the situation. Although short, the example follows the pattern of establishing a parent-child interaction for discussing the situation, exploring feelings, and providing reassurances and compassion through comfort.

EVALUATION

As a parent, why do I use this message?

I give my children big heart-to-heart hugs and tell them I'm giving you my love, do you feel it when I know they are struggling with a situation. I use this message because I want them to know that I care about what they are experiencing, I'm here to help them get through it, and I support them in their process. My hope is that they let me share in their experiences so that I can help them learn to manage their feelings. I want them to know that they are not alone in facing their fears and they can depend on me to support them through life.

As a child, what does this message mean to me and how does it make me feel?

It means that you are helping me not be scared or afraid because you are by my side. And, it makes me feel loved and happy. I feel it.

REFLECTION

What do I think about this message?

Take a moment to reflect on using the message, *I'm giving you my love, do you feel it?* Ask yourself:
➢ Does it help to build our parent-child relationship?
➢ Am I comfortable saying it out loud?
➢ Does it reflect a message that I want my children to understand and believe?
➢ Does it help me to encourage my children to be happy?
➢ Does it help me to alleviate my children's feelings of anxiety or sadness?

What intentional message will I use?

Based on your reflection, consider whether to adopt this message or to modify it for your use. If you chose something different, create your own message by writing it here.

I will comfort my children by saying …

Chapter 3
Reassurance

I'm always with you, in your heart and in your thoughts.

What is the message?

I'm always with you, in your heart and in your thoughts.

What is the purpose of the message?

The purpose of the message, I'm always with you, in your heart and in your thoughts, is to reassure our children that we are permanent and so is our love.

EXPLORATION

What is reassurance?

When we provide our children with reassurance, we try to *remove doubts or fears* they may be experiencing. As adults, we forget the many instances we faced as children; instances where we were afraid or sad in the absence of our parents. It can be challenging for our young children to tackle new experiences or face daily life, particularly when they are learning how to navigate in the world without us. Therefore, reminding them that they can think of us at any time may help them face the day.

Why is it important for my children to be reassured?

As with comfort, reassurances can help children decrease their distress and feelings of loneliness. We often need to remind them that we will be back to pick them up, when we leave them with caregivers or at school. Young children may struggle with understanding our permanence and therefore, may require many reassurances until they get it. But, we can also encourage them to develop their own method for self-reassurance by encouraging them to think of us when they need to feel that extra love and support throughout the day. By sharing with them that they always have access to us through their thoughts about us, we give them a coping strategy that they can readily access on their own.

What are the benefits of providing reassurance to my children?

All parents, at some point, leave their children in the care of someone else. Many children adjust rather well to the experience, however, some children consider this experience as painful or stress-provoking. Reassuring them of our return is crucial. Yet, we can go farther by giving them a strategy that allows them to cope with our absence. In this case, they are able to call upon that love, as a stress management and/or coping technique and remind themselves, that we will in fact, return. So, the absence is not permanent. In the event of parental death, this coping strategy encourages children to tap into their memories and feelings of love for us at any time, which hopefully provides them some comfort during their grief process.

If I encourage my children to think of me, will I make them miss me more?

By telling our children that I'm always with you, in your heart and your thoughts, we are not encouraging them to think of us all the time. We are encouraging them to know that we exist and if they need us, they can think of us to get them through the day. This will not make them miss us more or less, but it may provide them with some support and comfort, when they need it.

IMPLEMENTATION

When do I tell my children, I'm always with you, in your heart and in your thoughts?

This message is most appropriate in situations where there will be a separation or absence between parent and child, particularly for young children. Therefore, it is typically used when our children are struggling with separation and questioning our permanence. Telling them that I'm always with you, in your heart and in your thoughts, is a great way to part ways and allow them to remember that they only have to think of us to be close to us.

How do I use the message – I'm always with you, in your heart and in your thoughts?

This message serves as a reminder to our children that they have access to us whenever they need through their thoughts about us. They are able to think of our love or support whenever they want to. The message can accompany a discussion of their feelings and thoughts regarding the separation and can help to build the parent-child relationship by reaffirming our love for them.

The following example uses this message in a common situation where a child does not want to go to school due to the separation from their parents.

Example Scenario

Example situation.
4 year old child doesn't want to go to school.

Example reaction-interaction.
Parent: Tell me why you don't want to go to school.
Child: I don't like it.
Parent: What don't you like about it?
Child: I don't know.
Parent: Is there anything that you do like about going to school?
Child: Yes. Playing, learning, music, art.
Parent: What about seeing your friends; do you like that?
Child: Yes.
Parent: So, it sounds like you really like school and playing with your friends. Can you tell me what you don't like?
Child: I want you.
Parent: Oh, so you really like school but you don't like that I'm not there. Is that right?
Child: Yes.
Parent: I may not be able to be with you at school, but, I want you to know that you can think of me any time during the day and remember that I'll be back to get you. I'm always with you, in your heart and in your thoughts. All you have to do is think of me and remember my love. Remember that I'll be excited to see you and

hear all about your day when we are back together again. Does that make you feel better?
Child: Yes.
Parent: Will you try it out for today and tell me if it works?
Child: Yes.

The above example demonstrates that exploration is important in determining what is going on with a child. It is extremely common for children to state that they don't like something, however, upon further examination, there is another underlying issue causing their ill feelings. For instance, school. How many children don't like school? I ponder this often as I've discovered with my own children that it was either the separation from me or the dreaded naps that were the problems; not school itself. Through discussion and questioning, we can uncover the root of what is unpleasant and address it in order to remedy the underlying issues.

EVALUATION

As a parent, why do I use this message?

I tell my children that I'm always with you, in your heart and in your thoughts to give them the extra support, comfort and reassurance that although we may be apart, they can call upon my love by thinking of me. I want them to be able to control their own fears and doubts by using the love in our relationship to make them feel secure and happy. And, I want them to know that although I may not be in their presence physically, my love is permanent and with them always.

As a child, what does this message mean to me and how does it make me feel?

It really does help me because I feel you in my heart, I feel like I'm always loved, and I know that at the end of the day, I will see you again.

REFLECTION

What do I think about this message?

Take a moment to reflect on using the message, *I'm always with you, in your heart and in your thoughts.* Ask yourself:
> ➢ Does it help to build our parent-child relationship?
> ➢ Am I comfortable saying it out loud?
> ➢ Does it reflect a message that I want my children to understand and believe?
> ➢ Does it help me to encourage my children to be happy?
> ➢ Does it help me to alleviate my children's feelings of anxiety or sadness?

What intentional message will I use?

Based on your reflection, consider whether to adopt this message or to modify it for your use. If you chose something different, create your own message by writing it here.

I will provide reassurance to my children by saying …

Chapter 4
Belonging

I love that you are a part of this family.

What is the message?

I love that you are a part of this family.

What is the purpose of the message?

The intent of the message, I love that you are a part of this family, is to promote feelings of belonging in our children.

EXPLORATION

What is belonging?

People, of all ages, want to feel a sense of belonging in their lives. We want to *be a member or a part of something bigger*; therefore, we seek out groups, organizations, and/or communities that fit our needs. Belonging to these larger communities provide us with a way to feel accepted and appreciated for our interests, knowledge, beliefs, values, and/or opinions; positively affecting our lives and contributing to our overall health and happiness.

Why is it important for my children to feel like they belong in a family?

Maslow (1943) identified belonging as a necessary component in human motivation in order for people to thrive. Developing a sense of belonging in our children confirms that without them, the family would not be the same and therefore, their sheer existence has benefitted the family as a whole. When our children feel as if they belong as part of the family; they feel loved, valued, accepted, and appreciated for who they are as a person and how they contribute to the bigger system. These feelings promote positive health and happiness.

What are additional benefits for creating a sense of belonging for my children?

Belonging solidifies our child's place in the family as a permanent member and integral part of the family system, promoting a sense of security for each person. It reinforces an environment of love whereby the family is a solid unit or team, unique from other families, and a place that we call our own. It highlights the family as a system whereby each person plays an important part, has a specific purpose, and contributes to the overall success of the entire unit. Each member contributes to the greater good of the family.

Additionally, fostering a sense of belonging encourages our children to seek asylum from the uncertainties of their place in the world by reminding them that they have a place in their family of origin. Since the family is the first group a child belongs to, a good experience can encourage a healthy application of belonging through appropriate social interactions with other groups as our children expand beyond our family unit to participate in other organizations and systems. If our children understand that their participation is valued and important to our family, they can apply that in other areas of their lives, encouraging healthy interactions and participation in social groups for a lifetime.

IMPLEMENTATION

When do I tell my children, I love that you are a part of this family?

This message can be used at any time but is increasingly effective when our children need extra security and encouragement that promotes their self-worth as part of the family. When children are feeling like they are unsure of their place in the world, at school, or as part of a team, we can remind them that they belong to a family unit whereby they are valued and important.

How do I use the message – I love that you are a part of this family?

Using this message to foster a sense of belonging and promote our child's security in a system reminds our children that we each play a role in the family system and that each role is equally important, for without one of us, the dynamics of the entire system changes. Having conversations and facilitating dialogue whereby we point out the importance of each person, our gratitude for their existence, and their role in the family unit, is powerful for young children. They truly feel proud to be a part of something bigger than themselves. The discussion doesn't have to be long to be effective in reinforcing that our children are loved by all within the system. Bedtime is a good time to remind them of their importance and place in the family.

Example Scenario

Example situation.
6 year old child bedtime discussion with a parent.

Example reaction-interaction.
Parent: Have I told you lately, I love that you are part of this family?
Child: No.
Parent: Well, I do. You being part of this family makes it more special.
Child: You think so?
Parent: Yes. I believe that you help this family by being who you are. If you were not here, things would certainly be different and we would all miss out. Never doubt that we all love you and that you play an important part of this family. We are grateful that you belong to us.
Child: I love being a part of this family, too. I'm glad everyone loves me here.
Parent: I'm glad, too.

Although a brief interaction, it contains a powerful message – our children belong with us and in our families. Reminding them of this reinforces a loving home environment, contributing to their health and wellbeing. And, it makes children happy. At bedtime, that's an added bonus for sweet dreams.

EVALUATION

As a parent, why do I use this message?

I tell my children that I love that they are part of this family to reinforce my gratitude and love for them and to showcase that each and every member of our family is significant and valued as part of the entire system. I want to make a point to my children that no matter where they are in the world, they will always belong somewhere, specifically here, as part of this family. And, I hope that this encourages them to be active and positive participants in the other teams, organizations, groups, or systems they join throughout their lives.

As a child, what does this message mean to me and how does it make me feel?

It makes me feel happy because I'm part of this family and I know that everybody in this family loves me.

REFLECTION

What do I think about this message?

Take a moment to reflect on using the message, *I love that you are a part of this family.* Ask yourself:
- ➢ Does it help to build the family system?
- ➢ Am I comfortable saying it out loud?
- ➢ Does it reflect a message that I want my children to understand and believe?
- ➢ Does it help me to encourage my children to be happy?

> ➤ Does it help me to alleviate my children's feelings of anxiety or sadness?

What intentional message will I use?

Based on your reflection, consider whether to adopt this message or to modify it for your use. If you chose something different, create your own message by writing it here.

I will foster a sense of belonging in my children by saying …

Discussion ~ Love

The intentional messages in this section, which promote unconditional love, comfort, reassurance, and belonging, encourage love. When we create a home and family environment for our children based on love, we provide our children with the best opportunity for a healthy and happy childhood. We give our children a safe, nurturing environment where they can be who they are and explore who they will become.

Love is the basis for all that is good. We all strive for love. Love gives us hope, courage, calm, health, and joy. It keeps us going in challenging times. It makes good times even better. Thus, promoting love within our children is the greatest, foundational gift we can give to them, to ourselves, and to the world. The world could use more good. And, we could all use more love.

Part 2 ~ Confidence

Intentional Messages That Cultivate Confidence

Intentional Messages That Cultivate Confidence

Confidence – a feeling of self-assurance arising from an appreciation of one's own abilities or qualities (Oxford Living Dictionaries)

What is confidence in children?

For the purposes of this book, confidence refers to the self-confidence or self-esteem – *belief in one's abilities, worth or qualities* – of our children. Characteristics typically associated with confident adults include the way they look, such as having poise, using eye contact, and being polished in their appearance; and the way they conduct themselves, such as standing up for others, doing the right thing, and being decisive (Evrard, 2019; Top Tier Leadership, 2019).

Confidence in children may be harder to recognize if we only focus on the appearance. Yet, confident children conduct themselves similar to confident adults in that they are more likely to stand up for others, do what's right (most of the time; they are still learning), and make good choices. Confident children also overcome their fears in order to try new things, make new friends, and begin to form their own judgements about what's right and wrong in the world around them.

How do I cultivate confidence in my children?

Parents play a crucial role in facilitating the development of self-confidence in our children. Research shows that self-confidence exists in primary-school children, impacting student achievement, and is influenced by parents (Kleitman & Moscrop, 2010). Parents can plant the seed for which self-confidence in our children will not only grow, but flourish. We simply believe in our children until they believe in themselves.

Why cultivate confidence using intentional messaging?

Self-confidence is intimately personal and takes time to develop. Consider, it often takes a series of successes to become confident and only one failure to feel insecure again. As our children are learning constantly, their failures are more plentiful than their successes. Thus, cultivating self-confidence in our children requires an intentional strategy that can be used in a consistent and repetitious manner.

As with love, using clear, deliberate words to introduce and remind children to believe in themselves is an easy place to start. Intentional messages that stimulate the development of self-confidence in our children encourage them to try new things, explore who they are, and stand up for what is right – all qualities that promote healthy, happy lives. It also contributes to their academic and personal growth, ultimately, promoting their overall success because esteem is part of Maslow's (1943) hierarchy, required for children to attain success in life. Hence, when young children believe in themselves, they become limitless and are allowed to develop into the best version of themselves.

Let's explore the confidence messages that help our children to believe in themselves.

Chapter 5
Self-Belief

I believe in you, now believe in yourself.

What is the message?

I believe in you, now believe in yourself.

What is the purpose of the message?

The purpose of the message, I believe in you, now believe in yourself is to instill self-belief in our children.

EXPLORATION

What is self-belief in children?

There is a general consensus that *children's beliefs about themselves, or self-beliefs, are vital to their successes and failures* in all areas of their lives because what they believe to be true of themselves directs their actions and efforts (Pajares & Schunk, 2002). These beliefs, whether or not true, are perceived as true for children; therefore, if they believe they are good, they are more likely to act that way. Consequently, if they believe they are bad, their actions will reflect that, too. Thus, self-belief often equates to self-worth and therefore, is important to childhood development and is crucial to the development of self-confidence.

Why encourage my children to believe in themselves?

If we tell our children that they are good, they believe us until their experiences in life indicate otherwise. Yet, even if their experiences make them doubt their abilities, through messaging, we can remind them that they are good and worthy. If we truly believe in them, we can help them to build the positive beliefs in themselves. By telling them that we believe in them, we are taking the time to lay the foundation for goodness in them, and helping them to establish positive self-belief. Having a positive self-belief allows children to have positive feelings about their worth and qualities so that they will take risks, enjoy learning, and build confidence.

What is the parental role in cultivating self-belief for my children?

As adults, self-belief is internal (intrinsic) and has adjusted over time due to years of self-exploration and experiences. Children, however, have limited exploration experiences to build belief in themselves. As such, they require external (extrinsic) encouragement in order to begin to understand how to develop self-belief. The concept is rather complex but the process by which parents can help children to recognize self-belief is relatively easy. Simply pointing out that it exists is a great way for children to begin to understand and develop self-belief. Additionally, without parental guiding forces to provide them with encouragements, their doubts and fears reign supreme, setting up beliefs that are more challenging to overcome.

If I encourage my children to believe in themselves and they fail, won't they be disappointed?

When children fail, disappointment follows regardless of if we have encouraged their self-belief or not. Failure does not equal incompetence. Failure is expected as children are attempting new tasks and is oftentimes, required for learning to occur. Therefore, as children are exploring the world and trying new things, we must reassure them of their attributes and capabilities, while we encourage them to try their best and learn from their mistakes.

Additionally, failure does not create negative self-beliefs. Negative self-beliefs are created by the harmful and damaging thoughts that we believe to be true in our own minds. Negative self-beliefs limit our children, causing them to doubt their self-worth, avoid experiences or develop anxiety when attempting challenges. Consequently, telling them that we believe in them and encouraging them to believe in themselves is most beneficial as a remedy to failure and harmful thoughts.

IMPLEMENTATION

When do I tell my children, I believe in you, now believe in yourself?

This message is typically used when children are doubting their self-worth, viewing themselves in a negative manner, altering an undesirable behavior, or attempting tasks they fear. This message is also valuable when children are beginning to develop independence since parents are encouraging them to complete tasks for themselves by reminding them of their capability. Example situations include meeting new friends and/or teachers, attending camp (school, a party, or event, etc.), and changing behaviors.

How do I use the message – I believe in you, now believe in yourself?

Telling children I believe in you, now believe in yourself is best accompanied by an explanation about how believing in themselves is important for their lives and gives them courage. It is helpful to ascertain how children feel about a situation and discuss how self-belief can grant them the confidence needed to take the risk or make a change. For example, the message, I believe in you, now believe in yourself provides them with a dose of encouragement to gain independence, participate in experiences, and change unacceptable behaviors.

The following example uses this message when discussing zoo camp with a child.

Example Scenario

Example situation.
4 year old child going to zoo camp for the first time.

Example reaction-interaction.
Parent: Zoo camp starts tomorrow. Are you ready?
Child: Kind of.
Parent: Why, kind of?
Child: I don't know.
Parent: Are you nervous some?
Child: Yes
Parent: Tell me why.

Child: I'm scared that I won't know anyone.
Parent: You probably won't know anyone at first so that makes it a great opportunity to make new friends.
Child: Really?
Parent: Yes. Tell me, what makes you afraid when you don't know anyone?
Child: I don't know. It is something new.
Parent: That's true. It is something new which can be a bit scary and also exciting. Are you excited about going to zoo camp, too?
Child: Yes.
Parent: What are you most excited about?
Child: Seeing all of the animals.
Parent: We often have to work through our fears in order to choose to have fun. We can do that by believing in ourselves. You will get to see all the animals that you are so excited to see and you can meet new people, too. Doesn't that sound like something you want to do?
Child: Yes.
Parent: Well, I believe in you, now believe in yourself. Ready for tomorrow?
Child: Yes!

Parents sometimes fear that asking children if they are nervous or scared will make them that way. That is not the case. If children are not scared, they will say so. But if they are afraid, by asking them, we are encouraging them to identify their feelings, connecting those feelings to the underlying issues, and normalizing the experience. Discussing feelings is beneficial for emotional identification and development. Therefore, in the above example, talking about the feelings associated with the situation and providing encouragement is beneficial in helping the child to rise to the challenge.

EVALUATION

As a parent, why do I use this message?

When I tell my children that I believe in you, now believe in yourself, my hope is that they take my belief in them and internalize it. I want them to use the message as encouragement to participate in something new, push through something challenging, and embrace the opportunities before them. I want them to truly believe that they are good people, using this to combat any negative thoughts and feelings. And, I want them to be secure in who they are and know that through failures they will learn and through learning they will grow and through growth they will be happy.

As a child, what does this message mean to me and how does it make me feel?

It makes me feel like you believe in me, are always by my side, that I can do anything, and that I can trust in myself.

REFLECTION

What do I think about this message?

Take a moment to reflect on using the message, *I believe in you, now believe in yourself*. Ask yourself:
- ➢ Does it reflect my belief in my children?
- ➢ Does it help to build our parent-child relationship?
- ➢ Am I comfortable saying it out loud?
- ➢ Does it reflect a message that I want my children to understand and believe?

> ➢ Does it help me to encourage my children to be happy?
> ➢ Does it help me to alleviate my children's feelings of anxiety or sadness?

What intentional message will I use?

Based on your reflection, consider whether to adopt this message or to modify it for your use. If you chose something different, create your own message by writing it here.

I will cultivate self-belief in my children by saying ...

Chapter 6
Self-Efficacy

You can do this.

What is the message?

You can do this.

What is the purpose of the message?

The purpose of the message, you can do this, is to inspire our children to develop self-efficacy.

EXPLORATION

What is self-efficacy in my children?

Generally defined, self-efficacy refers to *the belief in one's capabilities to complete tasks.* Although self-efficacy is a "judgment of capabilities" not self-worth (Bandura, 2006), it, too is important to the development of self-confidence and self-esteem. If children believe that they can do something, chances are they will be right. And, if they believe that they can't, chances are, they'll be right, too. Thus, children who develop self-efficacy are able to access their fullest potential because when children believe in their capabilities, anything is possible.

Why cultivate self-efficacy in my children?

Henry Ford stated, "Whether you think you can or you think you can't – you're right!" Self-efficacy has become a central focus in educational settings because it is instrumental in predicting "motivation, emotion, and performance" (Bong & Skaalvik, 2003). Children who believe in their capabilities will naturally have more positive beliefs about themselves. As they grow, belief in their capabilities helps them to attempt new tasks, engage in experiences, and develop into independent, confident children. Therefore, parents can foster self-efficacy by believing in our children's capabilities until they believe in it themselves.

If my children fail, will they doubt their capabilities?

Fear and doubt are natural responses to failure. These emotions can damage our children's beliefs in their capabilities, potentially limiting their willingness to participate in future experiences. Yet, as parents, we possess the antidote to these damaging emotions which is learning. It is important to understand that failure is expected; children learn from failures; and learning is required for growth. Thus, it is advantageous to inspire our children to develop a love of learning so that failure is not the focus, learning is. When we expect failure as part of the learning process, fear and doubt are no longer the accepted response.

How does a love of learning help my child to develop self-efficacy?

Embracing learning as the cornerstone of growth is a powerful strategy for ourselves and our children. Homework offers us an opportunity to share a love of learning with our children. We can present homework as a positive event, a way for them to showcase their learning to us. In doing so, we demonstrate that learning is important to us and should be important to them. Additionally, we can teach children about learning itself. We can explain that learning is a process that requires effort (Brocato et al., 2018; McGuire, 2015; Brown et al., 2014) and is continuous and endless; therefore, the development of their abilities is continuous and endless, as long as they believe they can do it.

IMPLEMENTATION

When do I tell my children, you can do this?

This message is most useful when trying to help the child push through self-doubts in order to believe in their capabilities to complete tasks, whether those tasks are new, difficult, or even unpleasant. By saying, "You can do this," we are acknowledging that, in spite of any uncertainty, the effort of trying is more important than sitting out an attempt. When our children don't try, they are certain to fail. But if they try, the effort of trying is significant and sometimes just as rewarding as the success of the attempt.

How do I use the message – you can do this?

Parents can begin by discussing why the child is uncomfortable or uncertain about attempting a task. We can remind them that if they believe they can, they will; and if they believe they can't, they won't. And, we can emphasize that the effort of attempting to do something and learning from the experience holds the value in that experience. This will help them to push through their fears in order to develop the necessary confidence required for continued growth. Additionally, as children age, we can alter the message so that they are using it themselves by stating, "I can do this!" This demonstrates how they can take an intentional message, adopt it, and use it as the foundation for their own self-talk.

The following example demonstrates a way to cultivate self-efficacy in children by telling them, you can do this.

Example Scenario

Example situation.
5 year old child taking their first math test.

Example reaction-interaction.
Parent: I see you have a math test this week.
Child: Yes.
Parent: How do you feel about it?
Child: I'm a little scared.
Parent: What are you afraid of?
Child: Taking the test. What if I don't get them right?
Parent: It's okay to make mistakes; sometimes that's how we learn best. What matters is that you try your best. And, your test isn't until later this week so we have time to prepare for it. When you prepare, you start to feel better.
Child: Really?
Parent: Yes. You also need to believe in yourself. You can do this! I know you can. Don't you think so?
Child: I think so.

Parent: When it is time to take the test, I want you to close your eyes, take a deep breath and say in your head, "I CAN DO THIS!" Let's practice. Show me.
Child: (Eyes closed. Deep breath). I can do this!
Parent: Exactly. Now, let's review your math facts.
Child: Okay!

Remember to check in after the event to see if the message was effective. Like all of the intentional messages, repetition is important until they develop positive self-talk on their own. Additionally, children who adopt these strategies tend to share them with their friends, spreading positivity and confidence to those around them.

EVALUATION

As a parent, why do I use this message?

I choose to use the message, you can do this, as a way to help my children push through their fears and uncertainties in life as they are exploring new situations, tackling challenging ones, or trying to improve their skills. Self-doubt is a terrible enemy of self-confidence. Learning, however, is its truest friend. Because I want my children to be confident in their beliefs about their capabilities through learning, I choose to encourage them through the trials and tribulations of childhood, until they learn to encourage themselves on their own.

As a child, what does this message mean to me and how does it make me feel?

It makes me feel confident. If I'm scared to do something, it makes me feel less scared. And, if I think I can, I really can do it.

REFLECTION

What do I think about this message?

Take a moment to reflect on using the message, *you can do this*. Ask yourself:

> ➤ Does this reflect my belief in my children?
> ➤ Does it help to build our parent-child relationship?
> ➤ Am I comfortable saying it out loud?
> ➤ Does it reflect a message that I want my children to understand and believe?
> ➤ Does it help me to encourage my children to be happy?
> ➤ Does it help me to alleviate my children's feelings of anxiety or sadness?

What intentional message will I use?

Based on your reflection, consider whether to adopt this message or to modify it for your use. If you chose something different, create your own message by writing it here.

I will cultivate self-efficacy in my children by saying …

Chapter 7
Self-Image

Be the best you that you can be!

What is the message?

Be the best you that you can be!

What is the purpose of the message?

The purpose of the message, be the best you that you can be, is to stimulate the development of a positive self-image within our children.

EXPLORATION

What is self-image in children?

Self-image, or *the way a child views themselves*, also contributes to the development of self-esteem and self-confidence. Much the same as self-belief, our children's self-image affects the outcomes of life, both successes and failures, guiding their actions, feelings, and thoughts. Therefore, children with a positive self-image will live up to that image with their actions, feelings and thoughts; and conversely, those with a negative self-image will live down to those expectations, too.

Why is exploration necessary to cultivate a self-image?

It is difficult to truly value who we are and what makes us unique without first knowing who we are and what makes us unique. Building a positive self-image in children, requires us to first help them gain self-awareness through exploration. As they are trying new activities and learning constantly, children are finding what they like and don't like, what they are naturally good at and what requires practice. As they explore, they learn what makes them special or unique. Through self-awareness, children can gain tremendous confidence in who they are – valuing their abilities and qualities, and developing their self-image.

How do parental views of children impact their self-image?

The way we view our children is crucial to the initial development of their self-image. We often share the views we have of our children with them whether intentionally or not. This is particularly evident by the way we describe them and through labeling, whether we are talking to them or talking about them to others. Consider how often we use adjectives to describe our children from the beginning of life, such as describing babies to be good, happy, fussy, or difficult. We do it when we talk about them as a whole and when describing their habits, such as their sleeping habits (good or bad sleeper) or eating habits (good or poor eater). These descriptions continue as the child grows and develops, describing them as they reach or don't reach anticipated milestones and as they meet or don't meet our expectations of their behavior. At some point, they may be labeled – in its simplest form – a good child or a bad child. This label becomes the foundation for how our children see themselves, creating their initial self-image and determining the course of their lives.

How do I encourage the development of a positive self-image in my child?

Children try to live up to our expectations of them. Therefore, if they believe that they are bad, fussy, and/or argumentative because they have been labeled as such, their behaviors will meet those expectations. Conversely, if they believe that they are good, kind, and/or happy; they will engage in behaviors that reflect that, too. These descriptions and labels often become their initial self-image.

Since it is common for us to describe our children and in some instance label them whether we mean to or not, why not use this tendency intentionally to create a positive self-image in our children? If the goal is to have a child that has a positive self-image, is kind and caring, and is generally happy; then, we describe them that way. Simply put, we label them as good children and watch them meet those expectations.

What if I label my child good but they misbehave?

Our children can be good children who misbehave and make mistakes. As a matter of fact, we expect that to occur as they are learning and developing. It is important to separate the child from the behavior by pointing out that they are good children who made a poor choice. Choices are easier to remedy as children will have plenty of opportunities to make better choices in the future. Changing whether they are good or bad people requires much more work and is daunting to overcome for a young child.

IMPLEMENTATION

When do I tell my children, be the best you that you can be?

This message is beneficial when encouraging the child to grow from their experiences. Whether we are discussing a success or a setback, pointing out that personal improvement is necessary to grow is important. By encouraging them to be the best version of themselves, this makes the message personal, which serves as a powerful motivator for them to reach their fullest potential. Therefore, if the goal is to encourage them toward continued growth, then urging them to be the best version of themselves will be effective.

How do I use the message – Be the best you that you can be?

Parents can begin by allowing children to imagine what their best version of themselves looks like and then explore it with them. Children then describe who they are, what makes them special and unique, what their interests and abilities are, and what is important to them. Parents can also contribute uplifting descriptions of the child to initiate the development of a positive self-image.

Some example questions to get started on this exploration, include but are not limited to – What makes you a good child? What is most important to you in life? What makes you special? What makes you different than others? What makes you happy? What do you like to do? Who do you want to become when you grow up? What is your favorite subject in school? What do others like about you? What is the best thing about being you? When you feel like you are at your best, what does that look like? – Be willing to sit in silence and let them think, explore, then come up with an answer. Believe it or not, young children can answer many of these questions with practice and discussion.

Additionally, by encouraging them to be the best version of themselves, they begin to understand that they are unique from us and that by controlling their actions, they can control who they are. This is a powerful concept that may require time to accept; therefore, repeatedly reminding them that they can strive for better versions of themselves is key. It is important to remember to distinguish poor choices from who they are as people. And, it is helpful to remind them that we love them no matter what and that we will support them through this process.

The following example demonstrates a way to cultivate a positive self-image in a young child by separating the behaviors from the child's self-image and encouraging them to become the best version of themselves possible.

Example Scenario

Example situation.
6 year old child reprimanded for interrupting the teacher.

Example reaction-interaction.
Parent: I received a note from your teacher saying that she asked you to leave the classroom today.
Child: Yes.
Parent: Tell me about it. What happened?
Child: I was talking too much.
Parent: Were you following the classroom rules?
Child: No.
Parent: Tell me about that. What rule weren't you following?

Child: I didn't raise my hand and wait to be called on before I started talking.

Parent: What was happening in class while you were talking?

Child: Ms. Oscar was talking.

Parent: Were you interrupting her?

Child: Yes.

Parent: How did it feel to have to leave the classroom?

Child: Not good.

Parent: When you talk without following the rules, who are you affecting in your class?

Child: Me, because I get punished.

Parent: And?

Child: Ms. Oscar, because I interrupted her.

Parent: And?

Child: (shrugs)

Parent: How about the other kids in the class? Aren't you disrupting their learning?

Child: Yes. Does this mean I am a bad kid?

Parent: No. You are a good child. Your choice to interrupt your teacher was a poor one and it affected everyone in the classroom. The great thing about choices is you have the opportunity to learn from this and make better ones. Tomorrow is a new day. It is my job to help you to be the best you can be. How do you feel now?

Child: Better.

Parent: Good. Now, I want you to try to make better choices at school tomorrow. Remember, you are a good child. Be the best you that you can be!

This example demonstrates how to separate a poor choice from labeling the child as bad. Approaching the situation this way, allows parents to remedy issues quicker while keeping the child's self-image intact. And, as children begin to understand who they are and who they want to be, knowing that they can strive to be the best version of themselves, allows them to focus on growth.

EVALUATION

As a parent, why do I use this message?

I want my children to understand that life is about learning and growing. We are never done exploring, shaping, tweaking, or honing our true beings. I want them to love themselves, accept themselves, understand who they are, dream of who they want to become, and work toward that goal, separate from me, in order to reach their fullest potential. I tell them to be the best you that you can be so that they become confident in who they are and embrace the concept of continuous growth.

As a child, what does this message mean to me and how does it make me feel?

I believe it means to be the best you that you can be. The best me is kind, funny, and loves my family and friends.

REFLECTION

What do I think about this message?

Take a moment to reflect on using the message, *be the best you that you can be.* Ask yourself:
> ➤ Does it help to create a positive self-image for my children?
> ➤ Does it help to build our parent-child relationship?
> ➤ Am I comfortable saying it out loud?

> ➤ Does it reflect a message that I want my children to understand and believe?
> ➤ Does it help me to encourage my children to be happy?
> ➤ Does it help me to alleviate my children's feelings of anxiety or sadness?

What intentional message will I use?

Based on your reflection, consider whether to adopt this message or to modify it for your use. If you chose something different, create your own message by writing it here.

I will cultivate a positive self-image in my children by saying …

Chapter 8
Self-Pride

Sing loud and proud.

What is the message?

Sing loud and proud.

What is the purpose of the message?

The purpose of the message, sing loud and proud, is to stimulate self-pride in our children.

EXPLORATION

What is self-pride in my children?

Children who feel a *sense of pleasure or satisfaction in themselves* typically due to their accomplishments exhibit self-pride. Pride is an emotion that directly contributes to the development of confidence in children. As children achieve the tasks they set out to accomplish, they gain a sense of gratification from their successes, which in turn, drives a desire to continue to attempt more tasks. In doing so, they become more confident in themselves and their capabilities. Pride helps to stimulate development through learning and engagement, making our children willing to actively participate in life.

Why encourage my child to develop self-pride?

The development of self-pride is interconnected to the development of self-confidence and self-esteem (Tracy & Robins, 2007). Very young children experience and recognize pride (Tracy & Robins, 2007), making it is an ideal concept for parents to intentionally develop in young children through the use of messaging. From early on, parents can not only point out the accomplishments but use the words pride and proud so that children identify the feelings associated with success. Ultimately, pride brings about happy children.

Is there a negative association with pride?

People who exhibit excessive pride are often described as arrogant or conceited as opposed to the "authentic" version whereby adjectives such as accomplished or confident are used (Tracy & Robins, 2007). Therefore, when we promote the development of pride in young children, it is important that we focus on the healthier, authentic version by praising successes without overpraising or embellishing the events surrounding the success or by putting others down in the process. This will allow our children to use pride in a positive and personal manner to develop confidence to a healthy degree.

IMPLEMENTATION

When do I tell my children, sing loud and proud?

This message is more limited as it pertains to a specific situation, singing, yet, can be adapted for relevancy. Children often need support for performance-related experiences, in which case parents can utilize a pride message more appropriate to the situation. However, since young children typically have the opportunity to sing in educational or community events or situations, this can be beneficial when inspiring them to embrace the experience. And, each time children have a performance opportunity, whether it is singing, dancing, acting, performing in sports or even on tests, encouraging them to have pride and do their best helps them to confront their task with intentional zest.

How do I use the message – sing loud and proud?

Young children can be nervous for performances. Therefore, we can begin by checking in with them regarding any situations we anticipate or sense will cause them distress. We can discuss what will happen in order for them to understand what to expect during the experience. We can instruct them to take deep breaths as a means to calm their nerves. Then we can encourage them to do their best and have fun – sing loud and proud.

The following simple example demonstrates a way to encourage self-pride in young children.

Example Scenario

Example situation.
3 year old child singing in the Prekindergarten graduation.

Example reaction-interaction.
Parent: Are you ready to sing for your graduation?
Child: I don't know.
Parent: What are you singing?
Child: I'm a Little Teapot.
Parent: Do you know all the words.
Child: Yes.
Parent: Where are you singing?
Child: In the gym.
Parent: Have you practiced there?
Child: Yes.
Parent: Good, so you are prepared. You know the words and where you will sing.
Child: Yes.
Parent: Are you feeling okay about it?
Child: Yes (but hides face).
Parent: It's important to do your best.
Child: Why?
Parent: Because it will be more fun if you do your best.
Child: Okay.
Parent: Remember to take a deep breath. And, sing loud and proud!
Child: Okay!

This is more impactful with a quick follow-up after the event by asking them if they felt like they sang loud and proud. Did they enjoy themselves? Were they happy with the performance? We can also share how proud we are of them and how proud they should be with themselves, introducing self-pride to them at a young age. An alternative to encourage the development of self-pride in our children is to simply tell them to *have pride*.

EVALUATION

As a parent, why do I use this message?

I use the message, sing loud and proud, as a way to ease the anxiety of performance situations in order for my children to have fun, embrace who they are, and feel confident participating in these types of situations. I believe that if I encourage pride in them, they will then enjoy accomplishments and develop good habits for approaching future tasks. This will lead to healthier, happier children who believe in themselves and take the risks associated with performance to feel the rewards of their accomplishments. I hope that they embrace who they are and show the world, free from fear and judgment.

As a child, what does this message mean to me and how does it make me feel?

This means that I will sing loud so everyone can hear me and I will be happy, too.

REFLECTION

What do I think about this message?

Take a moment to reflect on using the message, *sing loud and proud*. Ask yourself:
> ➤ Is it relevant for my children?
> ➤ Does it help to build our parent-child relationship?

- ➤ Am I comfortable saying it out loud?
- ➤ Does it reflect a message that I want my children to understand and believe?
- ➤ Does it help me to encourage my children to be happy?
- ➤ Does it help me to alleviate my children's feelings of anxiety or sadness?

What intentional message will I use?

Based on your reflection, consider whether to adopt this message or to modify it for your use. If you chose something different, create your own message by writing it here.

I will cultivate self-pride in my children by saying …

Discussion ~ Confidence

The intentional messages in this section, which promote self-belief, self-image, self-efficacy, and self-pride, cultivate confidence and improve self-esteem. Helping our children to acquire confidence is paramount to influencing their attainments in life as it directly contributes to their thoughts, actions, and emotions. And, we have the power to influence those thoughts, actions, and emotions in a positive way in order to prepare our children for later in life, aiming to avoid the pitfalls associated with late childhood and adolescence by using intentional messaging.

As parents, we want our children to develop into healthy and happy adults who value themselves so that they respect themselves and others respect them, too. Choosing to provide our children messages that cultivate their confidence, gives them the opportunity to explore who they are and who they want to be. Ultimately, if our children know who they are, believe in themselves and their capabilities, develop a positive self-image, and have pride in their accomplishments, they blossom into young people who make good choices and do what's right – hopefully, making the world around them a better place.

Part 3 ~ Happiness

Intentional Messages That Encourage Happiness

Intentional Messages That Encourage Happiness

Happiness – the state of being happy (Oxford Living Dictionaries)
Happy – feeling or showing pleasure or contentment (Oxford Living Dictionaries)

What is happiness in children?

Parents often say that we want our children to be healthy and happy, but how do we attain this outcome for our children? There are numerous guidelines on diet, exercise, and sleep in order to help us gain and maintain healthy bodies; yet, we lack recommendations on how to develop happiness. Still, we have come to understand that happiness is vital to our overall health, particularly our wellbeing. Therefore, we need effective strategies that focus on the development of happy children.

The emotional side of us, in general, is more challenging to describe, recognize, and grasp. For instance, we tend to misinterpret happiness, often associating it only with the short-term effects of fun. While fun is important, the underlying emotional state we seek for our children to gain is more stable and persistent, less fleeting. Therefore, when parents reference "happy" children, we are typically referring to *contentment*, even though we want them to have fun, too.

How do I encourage happiness in my children?

Promoting happiness in children is dependent on successful emotional development. Children must first recognize that feelings exist. Therefore, we can begin the process of emotional development by urging children to identify their feelings and the feelings of others. When children are able to recognize feelings and appreciate the importance that feelings play in their lives, then they begin to make the choice to seek happiness for themselves.

Additionally, we can guide our children to develop qualities that lead to healthy emotional growth by teaching them to adopt sound emotional habits that result in contentment. For instance, certain "heart" attributes such as zest, hope, and love are known to influence happiness, even in young children (Park & Peterson, 2006). Therefore, we can urge our children to embrace these attributes and others such as kindness and forgiveness to promote their happiness, minimize their sadness, and stimulate their overall emotional development.

Why encourage happiness using intentional messaging?

Happiness is attainable. Achieving sustainable, lifelong happiness requires intentional focus and purposeful attention. Without a doubt, our children will face adversities and challenges; therefore, by having a coping strategy whereby they choose to maintain happiness in spite of those obstacles, they will be able to persevere. Therefore, we foster happiness in our children by helping them to recognize it, develop it, choose it, and maintain it. We help them to recognize happiness through self-exploration and self-awareness. And then, we help them develop it, choose it, and maintain it by using intentional messages that inspire them to view happiness as possible, worthwhile, and necessary. Because, when happiness is a cornerstone of the emotional self, additional positive elements will be present as well – leading our children to engage in sound emotional habits and contributing to their overall mental health.

Let's explore the happiness messages that help our children to develop emotionally.

Chapter 9
Awareness

How does that make you feel?
How do you think they feel?

What is the message?

How does that make you feel? / How do you think they feel?

What is the purpose of the message?

The purpose of the message, in this case questions, is to encourage our children to develop emotionally by recognizing feelings in themselves and others.

EXPLORATION

What is emotional awareness in children?

As the main foundation for mental health, emotions play a vital role in human development because they lead to feelings. Although emotions and feelings are complex, they are important because successful emotional development allows us to understand human nature, relationships, and ourselves. The process of emotional development begins with awareness. This occurs when children are *able to identify emotions in themselves and in others*. Once they become aware of emotions, they can begin to progress toward understanding themselves, valuing others, and forming healthy relationships.

Why is it important for children to be aware of feelings in themselves?

Children experience the same emotions and feelings that adults do. However, parental assistance is required for them to recognize and understand feelings. Furthermore, the ability to control emotions and feelings is predicated on being able to first identify them. The process of identifying and regulating emotions is known as metaemotion. Children can learn about feelings at a very early age. If they learn to identify their feelings, they can then begin to identify why they feel the way they do, and rectify those feelings by either changing their thoughts or actions, or by controlling their emotions (regulation). Developing metaemotion leads to better outcomes in life, including both happiness and success.

Why is it important for children to be aware of feelings in others?

Children are egocentric whereby they view themselves as the center of the universe. While they are the center of *their* universe and sometimes *ours*, we can aid them with understanding and valuing others in the world by pointing out that others have feelings, too. Recognizing other people's feelings is the first step in developing empathy for others and appreciating the common characteristics they share with others. Furthermore, when we specifically discuss how our children's actions impact another's feelings (good or bad), they begin to understand how they contribute to others around them, either positively or negatively. Hence, this allows our children to move from being egocentric to altruistic, *showing concern for others' wellbeing*.

Should my children recognize my feelings, too?

Yes! When we acknowledge our feelings, we allow our children to learn from us. As the primary role models for our children, it is imperative that we identify our feelings, in real time, so that we demonstrate healthy emotional identification. Whether we plan to or not, our children see us at our best and at our worst. So they know we experience both positive and negative emotions. Yet, we can normalize feelings for them by sharing our feelings with them, as we model the emotional development we expect of them.

IMPLEMENTATION

When do I ask my children, how does that make you feel?

There are countless opportunities to explore feelings with our children, starting from a very early age. As infants, they can be taught the basic emotions of joy, sadness, fear, anger, disgust, and surprise. As they become toddlers, we can teach them about excitement, frustration, jealousy, shyness, and nervousness. And, young kids can learn about pride, worry, embarrassment, and annoyance. We often assume that kids do not understand when we use big words. Yet, contrary to that belief, when we use feeling words in the appropriate contexts, children understand them relatively quickly and begin to use them on their own. It is satisfying to hear a small child state, "I'm annoyed," because we are then able to have a conversation about it and teach them how to cope with their feeling, rather than attempt to guess why they may be acting up. Therefore, parents must pay close attention to our child's cues and ask them in various situations, "how does that make you feel" to facilitate a discussion regarding their feelings.

When do I ask my children, how do you think they feel?

There are also many opportunities to ask our children how they think others feel. Yet, it is particularly insightful when our child has wronged or righted another. Instead of telling them how we think the other child feels about the situation, we can ask our children how they think the other child feels. If our child is unable to come up with an answer, we can ask a follow up question, "do you think they are sad" (or glad, mad, hurt, etc.). They can agree or not but it helps to facilitate discussion until they become proficient at identifying the feelings of others. This process reinforces emotional development through awareness and helps our children move toward truly seeing others in an empathic and altruistic manner.

How do I use the messages – how does that make you feel or how do you think they feel?

As with the other messages, facilitating discussions with our children in key to teaching them about life. Emotional identification is the same. Therefore, parents can share with children our own emotions, ask our children how they are feelings, and ask how they think other's feel, all at purposeful times. In essence, we have deliberate conversations about feelings, using these message questions.

The following example demonstrates an opportunity to encourage emotional awareness through the identification of feelings of the self and others for a young child.

Example Scenario

Example situation.
3 year old child who wants to take another child's toy.

Example reaction-interaction.
Child: I want Tommy's toy train.
Parent: You do? Tell me why you want Tommy's toy train.
Child: Because it is yellow and makes a choo-choo sound.
Parent: That is really special, huh?
Child: Yeah.
Parent: If you think it is special and I think it is special, I bet Tommy thinks it's special, too. Right?
Child: Uh-huh.
Parent: What is a special toy that you have?
Child: My koala bear.
Parent: Why is your koala bear special?
Child: Because she sleeps with me and lights up.
Parent: If someone took your koala, how would that make you feel?
Child: Sad.
Parent: Why would you be sad?
Child: Because I wouldn't see her anymore.
Parent: True. So, if you took Tommy's train, how do you think he would feel?
Child: Sad?
Parent: Yes, Tommy would feel sad. Just like you would feel sad if someone took koala.
Child: Oh.
Parent: Feelings are important and we don't take other people's things that are special to them because that would make them feel sad. Do you understand?
Child: Yeah.

When we encourage our children to think about others, they learn to recognize that sometimes they must put other people's feelings before their own. The end goal is for them to become less self-centered and more respectful of those around them by developing emotional awareness.

EVALUATION

As a parent, why do I use these message questions?

It is important to me for my children to label their feelings so that I can validate that their feelings are real and allowed. When we deny our feelings exist or act as if they are unimportant, we often end up feeling worse about ourselves. I do not want that for my children. I want to give them every opportunity to understand and control their emotions and feelings so that they accept their feelings as part of who they are. At the same time, I want them to develop a respect for others to become caring, compassionate people who value and show concern for others by helping them to recognize that others have feelings, too. I hope that my children acquire healthy concern and respect for themselves and others.

As a child, what does the message (how does that make you feel) mean to me?

It means that you want to know what I'm feeling and why. It helps me to be able to tell you my feelings.

As a child, what does this message (how do you think they feel) mean to me?

It helps me to see how other people feel so I can try helping them or say sorry to make them feel better if I did something wrong.

REFLECTION

What do I think about this message?

Take a moment to reflect on using the question, *how does that make you feel* and *how do you think they feel*. Ask yourself:
> ➤ Is it relevant for my children?
> ➤ Does it help to build our parent-child relationship?
> ➤ Am I comfortable saying it out loud?
> ➤ Does it reflect a message that I want my children to understand and believe?
> ➤ Does it help me to encourage my children to be happy?
> ➤ Does it help me to alleviate my children's feelings of anxiety or sadness?

What intentional message will I use?

Based on your reflection, consider whether to adopt this message or to modify it for your use. If you chose something different, create your own message by writing it here.

I will encourage the awareness of feelings in my children by saying ...

Chapter 10
Positivity

Choose to be happy.

What is the message?

Choose to be happy.

What is the purpose of the message?

The purpose of the message, choose to be happy, is to encourage positivity and optimism in our children.

EXPLORATION

Is happiness a choice?

We are capable of being happy; yet not all of us engage in thoughts or actions that lead to happiness. Herein lies, the choice. We may choose to engage in negative actions and thoughts, whereby our feelings are affected negatively. Conversely, we may choose to *engage in actions and thoughts that lead to positive feelings, creating optimistic views and leading to overall happiness.* At any point, we can alter our thoughts or actions toward positivity to make us feel happy. Once we choose happiness, we typically persist there, creating a more positive self. That doesn't mean that external circumstances and life situations won't cause us to be sad, anxious, angry or afraid at times, but when we look at life in general, we will have a positive identity, describing ourselves as happy overall.

Why should I encourage my child to be positive?

While some people adopt a positive identity early in life, it takes an entire lifetime for others to be optimistic, and, still for some, this never happens. Additionally, people tend to experience a negativity bias, whereby we remember and give more weight to negative experiences, emotions, and information (Grenville-Cleave, 2012). Yet, as parents we have the opportunity to combat the negativity bias with positivity by encouraging happiness and optimism in our children, resulting in positive outcomes. First, encouraging positivity in our children leads to the creation of the positive self, allowing our children to identify as happy. Second, when our children have a positive identity they look on the bright side, viewing situations optimistically even when encountering challenging circumstances and exhibiting resilience whereby they bounce back from setbacks. Third, positive identity and optimism leads to problem solving. When faced with problems, optimistic children hope for a solution and understand that they are capable of regaining their positive position. This allows them to rarely accept problems as is and instead look for solutions that get them back to their positive realm. Cumulatively, these positive characteristics – positivity, optimism, resilience, and problem solving – leads to success.

How does positivity and happiness lead to success?

Feelings, along with thoughts and actions, lead to successes and failures in life. As previously mentioned, feelings, thoughts, and actions are interrelated and dependent on each other, creating a cycle of success or failure. In turn, the outcomes of success or failure also contribute to our feelings, thoughts, and actions. For example, if we are happy, we will think more positive thoughts, and engage in more positive actions, which will lead to more successful experiences, thus making us even happier. This cycle fortifies why people tend to experience either repeated successes or repeated failures in their lives.

Figure 2. Cycle of Success or Failure

The advantage of the cycle means that it can be interrupted at any point in order to change the pattern and/or trajectory. So, if children are on a negative thought-action-feeling-failure pattern, changing one area can help turn the cycle from a failure cycle to a success cycle by creating a positive thought-action-feeling-success pattern. Encouraging happiness is a great way to interrupt the negative cycle and set our children on the path toward success.

Isn't sadness important, too?

Sadness is just as important as happiness because it clearly displays the direct opposite of happiness; therefore, it is required for people to realize what happiness feels like. Imagine a world with no sadness. Although we assume it would be wonderful, how would we know what true happiness really is without it? Sadness also plays a vital role by revealing problems with our children. Our child's sadness indicates to us that something is wrong and allows us to help them remedy situations, actively encouraging growth and development. Therefore, before we encourage our children to be happy, we must first validate and explore their sadness by investigating the reasons or experiences behind it, and helping them to develop a plan to resolve the sadness and reestablish happiness.

What about other feelings?

All feelings are valid and each person will experience them during their lifetime. Therefore, it is important for us to validate our children's feelings by conveying to them that it is okay to feel sad, mad, frustrated, nervous, lonesome, etc. We must normalize feelings and explain that feelings occur to give us a glimpse into what is going on with us; whether as a result of an internal experience or how we are responding to our environment. This removes the negative influence to their self-esteem that some children experience when they believe their feelings are not valid. Believe it or not, children often think that it is bad to experience negative feelings such as sad or mad, which in turn creates additional unnecessary negative feelings. So, by normalizing and validating feelings we can teach children that all feelings are important because they are the result of circumstances. Feelings indicate when situations are right or wrong and help us to know how to appropriately respond to circumstances. Therefore, it is necessary to explore feelings with our children through honest and intentional conversations.

IMPLEMENTATION

When do I tell my children, choose to be happy?

This message is best used during times when children need to reengage their focus toward the positivity rather than staying in the negative. There are many opportunities that arise, such as when children are sad to be separated from us, upset about not getting their way, grouchy or frustrated for any reason. It is also beneficial to remind them from time to time that happiness is a choice and that they can control it by thinking happy thoughts or doing things that make them feel good about themselves.

How do I use the message – choose to be happy?

As is the pattern, an open discussion whereby we guide our children in identifying their current feelings and then explaining that those feelings are valid is a good place to begin. After exploring their feelings and concerns, we can direct them forward toward the positive. This allows them to focus on the future, move on from the struggle, and choose something positive.

The following demonstrates an example of exploring and validating feelings while guiding a young child toward choosing happiness.

Example Scenario

Example situation.
6 year old child who wants to sleep at a friend's house for the first time.

Example reaction-interaction.
Parent: Are you ready for your overnight at Kate's house?
Child: Yes. But I'm nervous.
Parent: Tell me about that. Why are you nervous?
Child: Because I've never slept at a friend's house.
Parent: What is it about sleeping at a friend's house that makes you nervous?
Child: You won't be there and that makes me sad, too.
Parent: Why do you think you are sad?
Child: Because I know I will miss you.
Parent: It is okay for you to miss me and be a little sad and nervous about it. I miss you, too, when you are not with me. At the same time, I want you to choose to be happy because I don't want you to miss out on the things you really want to do because you will miss me. You remember how happy you were when Kate invited you?
Child: Yes.
Parent: Do you still want to go?
Child: Yes.
Parent: Good. Will you choose to be happy?
Child: Yes, Mom. I will.
Parent: And, when I pick you up tomorrow, I want to hear all about it!
Child: Okay!

This is more impactful with a quick follow-up after the event by asking them if they missed us and simultaneously chose to be happy. Children typically report that both occurred but that they were glad they went in spite of being a bit sad because of the separation. The hope is that during the time apart, if they feel sad because we are not there, they will use the message, *choose to be happy*, to coax and soothe themselves into focusing on the good. It is also beneficial to point out how proud we are of them that they took a risk to do something they really wanted to do in spite of their reservations about the experience.

EVALUATION

As a parent, why do I use this message?

I remind my children to choose to be happy to help them develop positivity, optimism, resilience and problem solving skills. I hope that they choose to enjoy the experiences life offers by focusing on being happy so that they don't miss out. I also believe that children want to be in control. By telling them that they can choose happiness, they feel like they can control it and they are move likely to put it into practice. As a result, I've often noticed in negative situations, my children focus on the good instead of grating on the bad, which makes me believe that the foundation of happiness is present.

As a child, what does this message mean to me and how does it make me feel?

It makes me feel generous and strong and it helps me be happy because I feel like I can choose to be happy.

REFLECTION

What do I think about this message?

Take a moment to reflect on using the message, *choose to be happy.* Ask yourself:
> - Is it relevant for my children?
> - Does it help to build our parent-child relationship?
> - Am I comfortable saying it out loud?
> - Does it reflect a message that I want my children to understand and believe?
> - Does it help me to encourage my children to be happy?
> - Does it help me to alleviate my children's feelings of anxiety or sadness?

What intentional message will I use?

Based on your reflection, consider whether to adopt this message or to modify it for your use. If you chose something different, create your own message by writing it here.

I will encourage happiness in my children by saying ...

Chapter 11
Kindness

Kindness.

What is the message?

Kindness.

What is the purpose of the message?

The purpose of the message, kindness, is to encourage our children to be thoughtful and caring.

EXPLORATION

What is kindness in children?

Consider, we initially recognize young children who are kind as "sweet". As they age, some become less sweet; maybe a bit salty, spicy, or sour. For others, kindness grows with them and we see their kindness in different ways. For example, kind children *show care and concern for the people around them*. They ask about other's feelings, particularly when someone is sick or injured. They are more apt to apologize and take responsibility for their actions if they have wronged another person. They stand up for those who may be unfairly or unjustly treated, even in the presence of authority. They do what's right, even when they are interacting in a group. They embody a happy identity, putting positivity into the world. They are generous and thoughtful, demonstrating empathy for those around them. In short, they make the world a better, more pleasant place as they respect themselves and those around them.

Why encourage kindness in my children?

We often tell our children to stop a behavior, but seldom do we identify what behavior we want them to embrace. Providing our children with the lesson of kindness encourages them to adopt a principle belief, whereby their spirit is based on positivity and happiness. It allows our children to recognize how to behave ... in kindness. Consequentially, kindness becomes their way of life, allowing our children to grow and develop using a positive, happy mindset. When children feel good about themselves by being kind, they are more apt to be happy because they live a positive existence. Researchers describe the connection between kindness and happiness in what they call a "positive feedback loop", whereby momentum is built between the two concepts that feed off of each other and continue the positive direction (Aknin et al., 2012).

Additionally, kindness is highly connected to mindfulness. In order to be kind, children must be present and aware of what they are doing (mindful). Mindfulness-based kindness becomes a habit, leading to self-regulation whereby children are able to recognize and control their thoughts, feelings, and actions. Research on mindfulness-based kindness indicates a positive effect on the social development and learning of children (Flook, et al, 2014). Therefore, the simple principle of kindness can lead to the meaningful outcomes of social and academic success.

Are there other benefits to encouraging kindness in my children?

The hidden benefits of kindness comes in the forms of self-love and self-respect, leading to happiness. At some point, by reminding our children to be kind, we are not only encouraging kindness toward others but also toward themselves. Most of the time, the people we are hardest on, are ourselves. This leads many of us to allow others to treat us poorly because somehow we view it as acceptable or even deserving. However, if we remind our children to be kind; the hidden message is that they deserve kindness, as well. This helps to build their own self-worth, resulting in happier and healthier lives, built on love and respect.

If my children are kind, will they be targeted by children who are not?

The possibility of being teased by other children is not more or less likely to occur because someone is kind. Kindness is not a sign of weakness, rather it indicates strength. The strength lies in the child's ability to be present, accept who they are, and become cognizant of others as human beings who have feelings, too. Having a kindness-based mindset helps our children to control the way they treat others and themselves. Additionally, kindness should not be mistaken for putting other's needs ahead of our own because kindness is about knowing and honoring who we are, while remaining considerate of others, too. Teaching our children to respect others through kindness helps them to see that each life is important, resulting in the development of empathy.

IMPLEMENTATION

When do I tell my children, kindness?

This message is appropriate when young children address others in a coarse manner. It helps to encourage sharing, cooperation, and mindfulness. Additionally, it is beneficial early on because it will be needed in the later childhood years when they begin to bicker with one another, particularly among siblings. By gently calling attention to our child's ill-mannered behaviors, we initiate the discussion about the reasons behind the behavior. Inevitably, this leads to conversations about their feelings, thoughts and likely, finger-pointing. Yet, in the end, the conversations surrounding kindness allow us to delve deeper into the connections we have with our children.

How do I use the message – kindness?

When we instruct our children to embrace kindness through this message, we are telling them that they are not currently exhibiting kindness or we are reminding them that we expect them to be kind in a given circumstance. By doing so, we are asking them to meet our expectations and behave in a way that leans toward the positive. Therefore, we use this message and then have an open discussion about our expectations. We can also explore the underlying feelings that our child may be experiencing during the situation.

The following example demonstrates how to encourage kindness.

Example Scenario

Example situation.
3 year old who doesn't want to share their toys with another child.

Example reaction-interaction.
Parent: Please share your toys with your friend.
Child: I don't want to.
Parent: Remember, kindness.
Child: *Grunts.*
Parent: What's wrong?
Child: I don't want to share my toys.
Parent: Do you like having friends to play with?
Child: Yes.
Parent: Do you want your friends to play with you?
Child: Yes.
Parent: Then we have to treat them with kindness. One way to do that is to share. How do you think you would feel if Jamie had cool toys but didn't let you play with them?
Child: Bad.
Parent: So, do you think that Jamie may feel bad now because he doesn't get to play with your toys?
Child: Yes.
Parent: What do you think you should do now?
Child: Share.
Parent: Why?
Child: Because it is kind.
Parent: And, do you think playing together may be fun?
Child: Yes.
Parent: Great. Then, show Jamie what's so cool about your toys so he can have as much fun as you.
Child: Okay.
Parent: Thank you.

A follow up discussion after the experience can help to solidify the messaging. For example, after finishing the play session, we can ask our child if they enjoyed showing off their toys and playing with the other child. Then, we can point out how being kind allowed them to have fun. And, how it positively impacted both children by making the experience pleasant because kindness is contagious. Once simple act of kindness can spread, resulting in happiness all around.

EVALUATION

As a parent, why do I use this message?

Kindness is highly important to me because I believe it is the foundation for health and happiness. I'm particularly intentional in building kindness within my children due to the positive outcomes of social, personal and academic success associated with it. Additionally, I believe that by teaching them to embrace kindness, they will not only be kind to others but they will also develop kindness toward themselves. In my opinion, in an ever-changing world that dishes out negativity, they will need to rely on their self-worth and self-love to get them through. I think kindness is the key. My hope is that through a kindness-mindset, my children will have less anxiety and more self-love.

As a child, what does this message mean to me and how does it make me feel?

It reminds me to be kind to others, whether they are family, friends, or even other people.

REFLECTION

What do I think about this message?

Take a moment to reflect on using the message, *kindness*. Ask yourself:
> - Is it relevant for my children?
> - Does it help to build our parent-child relationship?
> - Am I comfortable saying it out loud?
> - Does it reflect a message that I want my children to understand and believe?
> - Does it help me to encourage my children to be happy?
> - Does it help me to alleviate my children's feelings of anxiety or sadness?

What intentional message will I use?

Based on your reflection, consider whether to adopt this message or to modify it for your use. If you chose something different, create your own message by writing it here.

I will encourage kindness in my children by saying ...

Chapter 12
Forgiveness

Quick to apologize. Quick to forgive.

What is the message?

Quick to apologize. Quick to forgive.

What is the purpose of the message?

The purpose of the message, Quick to apologize. Quick to forgive, is to encourage forgiveness, leading to reconciliation.

EXPLORATION

What is reconciliation?

We all mess up. We do things that hurt other people without intending to – maybe due to a moment of weakness; maybe because we didn't consider someone else's feelings. All people make mistakes; we learn from them; we grow; we do better in the future. Still, sometimes, adults don't think before we act. For our young children, they function this way the majority of the time because they do not yet understand how their actions affect others. They need experiences to shape them and parents to guide them.

When our children make mistakes, we expect them to apologize. Yet, while most parents deliberately teach young children how to apologize for their mistakes by saying "sorry", we may not intentionally teach children how to forgive. Forgiveness is an equally important part of the apology-forgiveness paradigm, resulting in reconciliation, *the restoration of friendly relations*. Forgiveness allows everyone in the situation to move on and grow from mistakes.

Why encourage my child to forgive?

Forgiveness has been linked to better health, both physical and mental. For instance, forgiveness contributes to adolescent happiness (Rana et al., 2014). While apologizing is an acceptable, and oftentimes expected, behavior, forgiveness is also considered a positive social behavior that allows us to move past transgressions, contributing to our resilience. The process of forgiveness allows us to restore order and lessen fear, leading to less anxiety and better mood, as resentment leads to unnecessary anger. Therefore, forgiveness is beneficial for successful social development and is necessary for health and happiness, particularly as it relates to maintaining healthy relationships.

What is the role of forgiveness in the parent-child relationship?

Forgiveness is instrumental in creating healthy relationships. Adopting an intentional message whereby we encourage children to own their behaviors (through apology) and absolve the other party (through forgiveness) helps our children to view the many sides of the relationship. Depending on the circumstances, sometimes our children will forgive and sometimes they will be forgiven, both of which are equally important roles. This helps them to understand that each person plays a crucial role in a relationship through the apology-forgiveness process.

Furthermore, it is vital that we learn to apologize and forgive in order for any relationship to endure. This is particularly important for the parent-child relationship. As with love, it is a reciprocal concept, meaning, forgiveness goes both ways. We not only need to forgive our children for their wrongs; but we need to ask that they forgive us as well. Much of the damage done to the parent-child relationship occurs when our children do not forgive our mistakes or what they view as our wrongs. They hold on to the negative experience, allowing it to fester and create negative thoughts and feelings – damaging the relationship. By teaching our children how to apologize and forgive, we acknowledge ill-feelings and help our children move past the moment, letting go of the negativity and restoring balance. Therefore, forgiveness becomes vital to the health and endurance of the parent-child relationship, making it an important lesson to introduce to our children when they are young.

Do apologizing and forgiving render poor behavior acceptable?

Encouraging forgiveness does not excuse poor behavior. Apologies must be meaningful, compassionate, and intentional. Knowing that forgiveness may be readily available does not give our children permission to make poor choices that are intentionally hurtful because they plan to say "sorry". It does, however, allow them to make mistakes and grow with the confidence that they can maintain relationships, while owning their behaviors.

Furthermore, forgiveness must be offered willingly for the benefit of all parties and the relationship. When offering forgiveness, children sometimes say, "it is okay"; but the fact of the matter is that sometimes the behavior is not okay. Therefore, saying so is accepting the poor behavior. The more appropriate response is, "I forgive you," which really means, "I choose to forgive you for this and move on." This allows the party who was wronged to willingly forgive in order to restore friendly relations while maintaining an equal position in the relationship.

What if my child doesn't forgive (or isn't sorry)?

Apologizing and forgiving are choices. In order to make these choices, we must first understand the events surrounding the situation thoroughly then decide to move past it based on our feelings about the situation. The same is true for our children but since they are at the beginning of navigating relationships, they require guidance, instruction, and support to learn about the roles they play in disagreements and how to apologize and forgive.

First, let's examine apologies. If our child isn't sorry, it may be because they do not understand that they were wrong in the situation. We can address this through teaching them about what behavior was unacceptable and how they are expected to behave in the future. Typically, once they understand the wrong, they are then willing to apologize. Another common reason children don't say they are sorry is because they determine that their action was acceptable based on their feelings of the situation. This means that they feel like their actions were justified. This underlying reason requires us to thoroughly explore the situation with them and then, teach them why their wrong is unacceptable, in spite of their feelings (*For example: We never hit someone, even if they took your toys*).

While apologizing is difficult at times, forgiveness is a perpetual challenge, even for adults. If our child doesn't want to forgive, it is typically based on the level of wrongdoing and how it impacted their feelings. This means that the more our child's feelings are hurt based on their perception of how much they were wronged, the less likely they are to apologize. Therefore, we help them by exploring their feelings, validating them, and talking out the wrongdoing with the other person. We encourage them to move on for the benefit of the relationship but not before they tell the person how they feel, particularly in a more serious situation. We can teach our children to vocalize their feelings as they offer forgiveness (*For example: That really hurt my feelings. I forgive you.*). Therefore, quick to apologize; quick to forgive is most appropriate for situations that are not so serious and do not require the time and attention needed for more hurtful offenses.

IMPLEMENTATION

When do I tell my children, quick to apologize; quick to forgive?

When we want to remind our children to apologize and/or forgive in a given situation, we can use this message. Similar to the kindness message, this message calls out a poor behavior without blatantly acknowledging the wrong. Children quickly understand that this message instructs them to apologize or forgive based on their role in the situation. Teaching children about forgiveness early on also demonstrates that they are important people in any relationship, equal to the others involved in that relationship. And, they understand that sometimes they will apologize and sometimes they will forgive.

How do I use the message – quick to apologize; quick to forgive?

While children easily grasp saying they are sorry as an apology, teaching them how to forgive can be a bit trickier. The easiest and most effective way to teach this message is through role modeling. We pair the message with our own apology or forgiveness, whichever is appropriate in a given situation. This demonstrates how to play an active and respectful role in the relationship through the apology-forgiveness process. It is also appropriate to demonstrate in a sibling relationship because there are many opportunities to teach them how to apologize and forgive.

The following example demonstrates how to encourage forgiveness.

Example Scenario

Example situation.
4 year old who played with and broke a vase.

Example reaction-interaction.
Child: I broke the vase!
Parent: Tell me what happened.
Child: I was playing and it broke.
Parent: Were you playing with the vase when it broke?
Child: Yes.
Parent: Are you supposed to play with it?
Child: No.
Parent: Why didn't I want you to play with it?
Child: Because I might break it.
Parent: And, what happened?
Child: I broke it.
Parent: Do you see why I didn't want you playing with it.

Child: Yes.
Parent: That vase was important to me.
Child: I know.
Parent: I'm sad that it is broken.
Child: I'm sad I broke it.
Parent: What can you do differently next time?
Child: Not play with your things that can break.
Parent: Yes. Quick to apologize. Quick to forgive.
Child: I'm sorry.
Parent: I forgive you.

Through questions, we allow our children to identify their own, poor choices. They are given the opportunity to tell the truth, own their actions, and learn from their mistakes. Because they know we value apologizing and forgiving, they are more likely to own their misdeeds through truth-telling, too. By stating our feelings, we show them that feelings are important. And, by forgiving them, we allow them to move past their poor judgment. The same would be true if we were apologizing and allowing them to forgive. After we apologize, we state the message and allow our children to forgive us.

EVALUATION

As a parent, why do I use this message?

Forgiveness is good for our wellbeing because it allows us to move past negative experiences to more positive ones. I want my children to own their mistakes and poor decisions by apologizing but it is equally important to me that they give others the grace of forgiveness when they are wronged as well. If we hope for people to learn from their mistakes and grow, we have to allow them to get past those poor choices by providing them with an opportunity to reconcile. It benefits everyone when we move forward in a positive manner.

As a child, what does this message mean to me and how does it make me feel?

This makes me feel better because I know that I can apologize and will be forgiven. When you forgive me, I feel loved because even if you are disappointed, you forgive me. It is important to me when you apologize because you are saying you are sorry and that others make mistakes, too. I forgive you because I know that you always forgive me, too.

REFLECTION

What do I think about this message?

Take a moment to reflect on using the message, *Quick to apologize. Quick to forgive.* Ask yourself:
  ➢ Is it relevant for my children?
  ➢ Does it help to build our parent-child relationship?
  ➢ Am I comfortable saying it out loud?
  ➢ Does it reflect a message that I want my children to understand and believe?
  ➢ Does it help me to encourage my children to be happy?
  ➢ Does it help me to alleviate my children's feelings of anxiety or sadness?

What intentional message will I use?

Based on your reflection, consider whether to adopt this message or to modify it for your use. If you chose something different, create your own message by writing it here.

I will encourage forgiveness in my children by saying …

Discussion ~ Happiness

In the ever-evolving world, whereby each day more people, including adolescents and children, report being depressed and/or anxious, it is imperative that we encourage positive emotional development such as positivity, optimism, kindness, and forgiveness in order to give our children the best opportunity to be happy. We must begin early so that children can recognize and accept the importance that their feelings play for future happiness. If our children struggle to develop happiness, even when they choose it, we can consult with a mental health professional for guidance and support.

By helping our children to understand their own feelings and the feelings of others, we provide the foundation for emotional maturation and intelligence. In order to create healthy, happy children, parents must first deliberately contribute to their emotional development. Using intentional messages that encourage happiness helps our children to recognize that feelings are critical to their success and gives them the opportunity to embrace a positive emotional identity. Life is unpredictable and our children will undoubtedly face adversities, therefore, it is important that we give them the tools they need to choose to be happy in order to protect them from despair. In the darkest of times, they will need this positive spirit to lead them back to the light.

Part 4 ~ Integrity

Intentional Messages That Build
Integrity

Intentional Messages That Build Integrity

Integrity – the quality of being honest and having strong moral principles (Oxford Living Dictionaries)

What is integrity in children?

Moral integrity is a defined pattern of choices and actions, pervasive and consistent over time. It is an underlying quality or characteristic we behold that directs us in our choices and actions. Integrity is a characteristic we either have or don't have, contingent on our ability to adopt it during our development. The same is true for our children. As parents, we serve as the moral compass for our children. Therefore, when we welcome integrity as our core foundational moral principle, we produce children who *bestow strong moral characteristics* themselves, recognized as virtuous.

While most children will attempt to lie or withhold information in order to prevent getting in trouble, children who are taught and accept integrity as a core foundational value, will do so less often. Children with integrity, will become the children who tell the truth when it matters most, even when it is trivial; stand up for others, even when it is unpopular; and do the right thing, even when it is uncomfortable. These children, in turn, set an example and become a moral compass for others, including their peers.

How do I build integrity in my children?

Parents, first and foremost, serve as teachers through role modeling. We model for our children the values, beliefs, and principles we embody each and every day. Our morals have merit, in the simplest of descriptors, strong or poor. Our moral fortitude extends to our children, whereby they mimic our behaviors. For instance, if we own our mistakes through honesty, so will our children. Conversely, if we tell lies, so will our children. While we can anticipate that our children will lie when learning to navigate the world, we can minimize and correct this behavior by teaching them that we fundamentally and primarily value integrity. In short, we model how we want them to behave with integrity through our own virtuous choices and actions.

Why build integrity using intentional messaging?

Research indicates that virtue contributes to peace and happiness later in life (Demirci & Ekşi, 2018); therefore, developing morality within our children provides them with an added foundation for the development of their health and happiness, allowing them to reach their fullest potential (Maslow, 1943). Our ability to raise our children to be virtuous and embody a sound moral compass is dependent on our ability to build integrity within them. In addition to being a good role model, we can build integrity in our children by teaching them how to make good decisions, be honest, be responsible, and own their mistakes, all of which are connected to the concept of virtue. We can do so by using intentional messages to consistently provide them with clear messages that demonstrate our expectations of their behavior.

When faced with situations that require our children to make challenging choices, they will use these intentional messages for guidance. This is especially necessary as they face peer pressures to gain acceptance or friendship. If they know how to behave in a kind and assertive manner based in integrity, they are more likely to make good choices, regardless of the pressures they face, while maintaining quality relationships with people who respect them.

Additionally, by building integrity within our children, we can protect them from creating a negative self-concept. The underlying negative impact of a lack of integrity through dishonesty or depravity, is shame. Therefore, by building integrity using focused, deliberate messaging we make a positive impact by instilling in our children the pride and security that results in self-love, self-respect, and happiness. And, by listening to the messages that build good character, our children rely on these messages to form their own value and belief systems, contributing to their overall development and encouraging them toward healthy and happy lives.

Let's explore the integrity messages that help our children to develop strong moral character.

Chapter 13
Decision Making

You are not bad; you made a bad choice.

What is the message?

You are not bad; you made a bad choice.

What is the purpose of the message?

The purpose of the message, you are not bad; you made a bad choice, is to teach children how to develop good decision making skills without damaging their self-concept.

EXPLORATION

What is good decision making in children?

As adults, we take for granted the complex process of making decisions, even the easy ones, because we have honed our skills and practiced often. Consider we make countless decisions each day, some easy; some less so. Only when we are faced with difficult decisions do we recognize that making decisions can be challenging. Yet, for our children, they are beginning to learn how to make choices. Even the simplest choice is *a complex process* for them that requires patience and guidance so that they can learn how *to make what we believe are good choices*.

Children who successfully learn good decision making will be those who attempt to make good choices and self-correct when they make poor ones, resulting in making better choices overall. We see this reflected in the outcomes of their decisions; what we know to be the consequences of their choices. Every choice has a consequence. We typically associate consequences with the negative but consequences can be positive. If we make a good choice, the result is a positive consequence; just as if we make a bad choice, the result is a negative consequence.

How do I teach my child to make good choices?

To foster healthy decision making in young children, we begin by giving them controlled choices so that they can experience autonomy. We control the outcome by limiting the choices to two options. This results in a child that is happy with what they get because they chose it and us happy with the outcome because we predetermined it as acceptable. For example, we may ask our child – Do you want an apple or an orange? Either way the child is getting a piece of fruit, which we predetermined is acceptable. They are happy because they get to pick which one they get. This is a simple exercise in encouraging our children to practice decision making. As they age, we expand the choice options in order to make the decisions more challenging yet more developmentally appropriate, until we allow them to make decisions on their own without limits. For example, in early elementary school, we may allow our child to pick which extracurricular activity they want to participate in after school by giving them four choices, all of which are acceptable to us. In later elementary school, we may encourage them to suggest to us an extracurricular activity they want to research and explore to participate in. They then present the information to us for approval.

Why encourage my child to make good choices?

Good decision making is the first step to build integrity. Research shows that moral characteristics are essential for ethical decision making later in life (Heyler et al., 2016). Before we know it, our children will grow and depend on their own decision making in order to navigate the world around them. Earlier than we anticipate, they will be faced with choices that have serious ramifications. If they are capable of making good choices, they will meet the challenge. If they are not, they will succumb to the consequences of poor decision making. A series of consecutive bad choices can have dire consequences. Therefore, it is imperative to teach our children how to make good choices; their future health and happiness depends on it.

Why does this message focus on poor choices?

While it is equally important to point out good choices through praise, the significance of this message is to separate the poor choice from a tendency to label a child as bad. A previously mentioned, we often hear children described as "such a good baby," or conversely, "so bad"? Labeling children as bad sets them up for acting according to that expectation. When we do so, we get more bad outcomes because they already believe that they are bad, even if our intent is to discourage their bad behaviors. We actually produce the opposite outcome. Yet, parents are sometimes surprised when our children live up to, or in this case, down to our expectations, particularly when we label our children as bad. Consider, if they already believe we think they are bad, why would they choose to act any other way?

Additionally, when we label our children as bad, they internalize that label and they believe us. Separating the behavior from the child allows them to recognize that they can change the behavior by simply making a better choice. It is much easier to change a choice than it is to change who we are as a person. Therefore, by separating the choice from the child, we allow our children to control the outcomes of who they are and will become. This prevents them from internalizing their mistakes and helps them to recognize that they can make poor choices, since they are still learning, while simultaneously maintaining their goodness as a child.

How does good decision making help my child to be healthy and happy?

Decision making is a process which requires deliberate practice and results in the development of a skill. This particular skill development is a lifelong endeavor that leads to independence and personal empowerment, which in turn, results in children who live up to their potential. When we couple good decision making with honesty and decency, we encourage the development of adults who thrive and are happy with who they are as people. In the end, this results in creating children who make sound choices that lead to their health and happiness. Furthermore, as parents, how do we know that our children are ready to embark into the real world? The answer is simply – when we know they can make good, healthy decisions on their own.

IMPLEMENTATION

When do I tell my children, you are not bad, you made a bad choice?

This message is best used when our child makes a poor choice, particularly if a punishment is necessary. As previously stated, when children are learning to navigate the world, they make many mistakes. Therefore, there will be a multitude of opportunities to explain that although they made a bad choice, they are not a bad person. As their teacher, we want to point out their missteps so that they learn from those mistakes. But, it is particularly important to use this message when they do something that either disappoints us or requires punishment. After discussing the situation that led to the punishment we can reassure them that the choice was poor and can be changed in the future; yet they are still good children.

How do I use the message – you are not bad, you made a bad choice?

It is important to call out the misbehavior and discuss why it is a poor choice. We also explain how we expect our child to behave in the future, given the same circumstances. When they get older, we ask them what they should have done instead. This encourages them to process their mistakes and reflect on the better choices that they can make in the future, allowing them to go through the decision making process without the fear of negative consequences, as they may already be in trouble. This conversation does not negate the need for punishment. There will be times that children misbehave enough to require punishment. But, it is in these times that we must reassure them that their core positive inner-being is still intact, regardless of their current choice.

The following example demonstrates how to build good decision making in children.

Example Scenario

Example situation.
5 year old who kicked their sibling.

Example reaction-interaction.
Parent: Let's talk about what happened. Tell me why you kicked your brother.
Child: He was ignoring me when he was playing his game.
Parent: So you were trying to get his attention?
Child: Yes.
Parent: I know you wanted him to talk to you but it is not acceptable to kick someone. What should you have done instead?
Child: I should have tried to get his attention another way.
Parent: Yes, tell me another way that you could have tried to get his attention.
Child: Maybe I could have called his name again.
Parent: Or?
Child: I could have put my hand on his arm and said his name so he knew I was there.
Parent: Yes, or you could have stood where he could see you and then talk to him.
Child: Yes.
Parent: You now have options next time you want to get his attention and he is ignoring you, none of which are kicking him.
Child: Okay.
Parent: You need to apologize to your brother for hurting him.
Child: Yes, ma'am.
Parent: How are you feeling?
Child: Bad.

Parent: Why?

Child: Because I did something wrong. Does this make me bad?

Parent: No. You are not bad, you made a bad choice. The great thing about choices – we makes lots of them every day. You make good choices most of the time. And, you now know what you should have done instead. So, you can choose to make better choices in the future, even when you are trying to get someone's attention.

Child: Okay.

Parent: How do you feel now?

Child: Better. Can I go apologize now?

Parent: Absolutely.

Through discussion, we allow our children to reflect on their poor choices and come up with alternative actions. They will have the opportunity to gain our expectations of them, understand what they did wrong, and recognize that their choice was bad but that doesn't mean that they are. Correcting poor behavior as choices also shows that our children are in control of their actions. And, it helps them to move past transgressions while keeping their spirit intact.

EVALUATION

As a parent, why do I use this message?

I believe that if we want to create good people, then we set the expectation that our children are good. Therefore, when they make mistakes, these choices may be bad, but that does not mean that my child is bad. I, particularly want to protect their self-concept – *how they view themselves.* So, it is important to me to ensure that each choice does not lead them to feel like a bad person, but that each choice can be made better next time, resulting in better choices in the future while maintaining good children in the process.

119

As a child, what does this message mean to me and how does it make me feel?

It means that even though I know I made a bad choice or did something wrong, I'm not a bad person.

REFLECTION

What do I think about this message?

Take a moment to reflect on using the message, *you are not bad, you made a bad choice.* Ask yourself:
> ➤ Is it relevant for my children?
> ➤ Does it help to build our parent-child relationship?
> ➤ Am I comfortable saying it out loud?
> ➤ Does it reflect a message that I want my children to understand and believe?
> ➤ Does it help me to encourage my children to be happy?
> ➤ Does it help me to alleviate my children's feelings of anxiety or sadness?

What intentional message will I use?

Based on your reflection, consider whether to adopt this message or to modify it for your use. If you chose something different, create your own message by writing it here.

I will build good decision making in my children by saying ...

Chapter 14
Honesty

Always tell me the truth.

What is the message?

Always tell me the truth.

What is the purpose of the message?

The purpose of the message, always tell me the truth, is to instill honesty in and develop trust with our children.

EXPLORATION

What is honesty in children?

The truth is that all children lie. Lying indicates that our child's brain, particularly their cognitive, thought processing, is maturing. As such, lying is a developmentally appropriate tactic children use to evade trouble, look better, or avoid hurting feelings. Likewise, these reasons typically explain why adults lie, too, although in a more sophisticated manner. If we accept that all children lie, we can anticipate and strategically correct it in order to inspire our children to become honest. Consequentially, if we fail to instill honesty as a foundational principle within our children, they will continue lying into adulthood, resulting in negative personal and social consequences, including potential mental health issues. Conversely, when children develop strong, positive morals, they feel good about themselves, leading to healthier and happier people who enjoy and maintain quality relationships. In short, honesty is the impetus for building integrity in children as it is the fabric for moral character construction. Therefore, honest children *tell more truths* and in turn, more people believe them.

Why encourage my child to be honest with me?

Encouraging our children to tell the truth is the gateway to forming the honest child. This is a necessary step in developing the strong moral character that we seek for our children to embody but it is equally important as the basis for our ability to protect our children. Consider that if our children are honest with us, when they tell us truths that result in our need to defend them or go to bat for them, then we can do so with confidence. There will come a time when we gain conflicting information from two sources; one from our child and another from someone else, possibly someone in authority. It is in these times, where we must be able to believe our children's word in order to properly serve as their defender or advocate, whichever parental role is applicable to the given situation. Alternatively, if our children are apt to lie, we may doubt their word as truth and in turn, miss opportunities to protect them, potentially causing more damage to our children and/or our relationship. Therefore, it is important when we encourage our children to tell us the truth that we explain that it is a necessary process in our ability to parent and protect them. We must also take it one step further and explain that because we expect them to always tell us the truth, we are committed to always believe them in return. This results in a parent-child relationship grounded in trust which is the essential core of any healthy relationship.

Why must I maintain honesty with my child?

As with love, honesty goes both ways, meaning while we expect our children to be honest with us, we need to commit to being honest with our children. Using intentional messaging is a useful application only if we are honest with our children because we are using words as a basis for communicating with our children in order to instill the values and principles that we believe are necessary for their successful development. If we ask for honesty from our children, but conduct ourselves in a false manner, they will quickly identify our deception, resulting in distrust. Therefore, our own words must be grounded in honesty to encourage the strong parent-child relationship and build the moral character we hope to inspire in our children. Simply put – if we want to raise honest children, we must be honest ourselves.

Is honesty always the best policy?

While ideally and usually honesty is the best policy, there are times when we find ourselves avoiding the truth in special circumstances. For instance, pure honesty can be socially unacceptable, particularly when it is unsolicited or impolite. Therefore, we must teach our children that at times, although they recognize their truth, it may not be appropriate to share. If they must share, they must be thoughtful in the delivery of the information in order to avoid hurting other's feelings. At times, this requires that people ask for their opinions, prior to offering these truths in order to avoid a social gaffe.

Additionally, there will be times when the truth is not suitable for our children to hear due to the gravity of the situation. If the truth is not acceptable for sharing with our child, then it is important to tell them so. For example, we can state, "I can't answer your question or tell you about this yet because I don't believe you are old enough to hear it. However, when the time comes that I believe you can handle the truth, I will share it. For now, I ask for your trust in me to know when to tell you." Children will trust and respect our judgment because of the honesty we exhibit when we choose to or not to explain these complicated situations.

IMPLEMENTATION

When do I tell my children, always tell me the truth?

Because honesty is a necessity for building solid relationships, this message can be used regularly and in a multitude of situations. However, it will tend to come up naturally and be most appropriate when we recognize that our children are struggling to decide whether or not to tell us the truth, when they lie to us, and/or when we tell them the hard truths (in an age appropriate manner) to the questions they ask. This message can also serve as a reminder that we expect honesty from them regardless of the situation.

How do I use the message – always tell me the truth?

It is important to explain that because we expect our children to always tell us the truth, that we will always believe them. Therefore, their word means something and they have control over what they say and contribute to how we respond. Consequently, their explanations of what occurs in a given situation are taken as truths. Only when we uncover the falsehoods with evidence should we ever questions their word and confront them about their deception. Using the intentional method in a way that continues to allow us to develop deeper relationships with our children through facilitated discussion is ideal.

Yet, when our children choose to lie, there must be negative consequences such as punishment. Therefore, in these situations, we can consider punishing them for lying instead of the original transgression in order to focus on honesty as the most important lesson in the situation.

The following example demonstrates how to build honesty with a young child beginning to lie.

Example Scenario

Example situation.
4 year old who spilled milk on the kitchen floor but didn't tell anyone.

Example reaction-interaction.
Parent: Oh my. Did you spill your milk on the kitchen floor?
Child: No.
Parent: Hmm. I wonder how it got all over the floor then.
Child: I don't know, Mom.
Parent: You don't? Are you sure?
Child: Yes.
Parent: Well, if you and I are the only two people in the house and I didn't spill it and you didn't spill it; then what happened?
Child: I don't know.
Parent: Are you sticking with that? Remember, always tell me the truth. Your word is the most important possession you own. And, it is important for me to always be on your side in order to protect you. There will be times when you will tell the truth and people may not believe you, but I will. You know why?
Child: No, why?
Parent: Because you always tell me the truth. That's why. So, if we agree that you will always tell me the truth, then we can also agree

that I will always believe you. This will help me to be able to protect you as your parent. And, that is very important for the both of us. Okay?

Child: Yes.

Parent: Is there anything you want to tell me?

Child: Yes. I spilled the milk.

Parent: Okay. Now, why didn't you want to tell me?

Child: Because I thought you would get mad at me and I'd be in trouble.

Parent: Then you were wrong. I won't get mad about spilling milk. Accidents happen and we can easily clean this up. I am upset, however, that you lied to me.

Child: I'm sorry.

Parent: I appreciate your apology. And, I forgive you. At the same time, I must punish you for lying because it is an important lesson for you to learn. Therefore, you cannot watch TV for today for lying to me. If you would have told me the truth, we would have just cleaned up the mess together and moved on. Do you see how lying is what got you in trouble when you were trying to avoid trouble by not telling me you spilled the milk?

Child: Yes.

Parent: What should you have done instead?

Child: I should have told you I spilled the milk.

Parent: Good. Now let's get this mess cleaned up.

Child: Okay.

Parent: I love you no matter what!

Child: I love you, too, Mom.

When children begin lying, it is often to avoid trouble for minor instances that would not have gotten them in trouble in the first place. It is a prime opportunity to punish them for lying instead of the original transgression and use an intentional method to encourage them to always tell us the truth. We can use multiple messages from the book and integrate them into the discussion. In this example, we forgive them for apologizing and remind them that we love them no matter what. It is important to remind them that their misdeed does not prevent us from loving them.

EVALUATION

As a parent, why do I use this message?

I believe that trust is the basis for all good relationships. Honesty brings about trust. If I am honest with my children, they will in turn be honest with me. If I expect honesty from them, they will learn to be honest. While pure honesty is not always socially acceptable, teaching my children how to be honest in a polite, respectful manner will give them a foundation for understanding how to deliver truthful messages in a kind way. In the end, I want my children to be honest so that they feel good about themselves and so that we can trust one another. In the end, I believe this will positively contribute to their morals and integrity.

As a child, what does this message mean to me and how does it make me feel?

It reminds me to always tell the truth and never lie because you won't trust me anymore.

REFLECTION

What do I think about this message?

Take a moment to reflect on using the message, *always tell me the truth*. Ask yourself:
- ➤ Is it relevant for my children?
- ➤ Does it help to build our parent-child relationship?
- ➤ Am I comfortable saying it out loud?
- ➤ Does it reflect a message that I want my children to understand and believe?
- ➤ Does it help me to encourage my children to be happy?
- ➤ Does it help me to alleviate my children's feelings of anxiety or sadness?

What intentional message will I use?

Based on your reflection, consider whether to adopt this message or to modify it for your use. If you chose something different, create your own message by writing it here.

I will build honesty in my children by saying …

Chapter 15
Accountability

If you're brave enough to do it, be brave enough to own it!

What is the message?

If you're brave enough to do it, be brave enough to own it!

What is the purpose of the message?

The purpose of the message, if you're brave enough to do it, be brave enough to own it, is to hold our children accountable for their actions by teaching them ownership.

EXPLORATION

What is accountability in children?

For the purposes of this book, accountability in our children refers to *the ability of our children to take ownership of their actions and behaviors* by holding them responsible for those actions and behaviors as their parental teacher. The child who adopts this principle of being brave enough to own their actions is identified through honorable behaviors. For example, the accountable child readily admits mistakes, candidly explains what happened, and voluntarily takes responsibility for the outcomes of their actions. Poor and/or naughty actions require discipline. Yet, children who accept responsibility for their actions are more likely to also accept disciplinary consequences as they understand that their actions led to those consequences. Over time, this results in children who refrain from engaging in negative behaviors because they begin to think before they act. Therefore, if they know they must own their actions, which will lead to disciplinary consequences, they choose not to engage in the poor behavior, resulting in increased self-control over their actions.

Why encourage my child to own their actions?

All actions have consequences, whether positive or negative. Through accountability, we can teach our children that while positive actions will result in praise and positive consequences, negative actions will result in reprimand and negative consequences. Both are equally important to the development of a healthy child. And, both require us to teach our children how to own their actions. While we want our children to gain glory in their positive actions, so, too, must we teach them to accept the results of their negative actions, which oftentimes is personal shame. Yet, when they own their actions, there is a sense of pride that accompanies accountability, making the shame less stinging.

Children who own their actions are better equipped to refrain from engaging in negative behaviors that can result in excessive negative outcomes in adolescence and adulthood. Instead, through accountability, our children will not only decrease negative behavior, positive outcomes such as self-control, honesty, and overall integrity will increase. This results in children who have good feelings about themselves, including self-love, and ultimately results in the development of healthy and happy children.

Why must I own my own actions with my child?

A prerequisite for building integrity in our children lies in our ability to model integrity in ourselves. This requires us to lead by example. Therefore, if we are brave enough to do something, we should be brave enough to own it, too. When we model such behavior, our children readily accept it as the standard operating procedure in life. Additionally, as we admit to our mistakes, our children also see that they don't have to be perfect, helping them avoid the pitfalls of perfection. Life is about continuing to learn and grow not only for our children but for ourselves. Thus, we must strive to get better each day in order to maintain and attain healthy and happy lifestyles. Still, we are fallible and will make mistakes. It is when we make mistakes that we contribute the most to our parent-child relationship because our children are given the opportunity to see our true being and our response to adversity. As a result, children feel empowered because they learn from, forgive, and love us as we are – just as we do with them.

IMPLEMENTATION

When do I tell my children, if you're brave enough to do it, be brave enough to own it?

There are numerous opportunities to use this message when our children are learning to navigate the world. They make mistakes often, providing us an opportunity to encourage them to own both good and poor actions. Each time we choose to use this message, particularly when they make mistakes, we build integrity within our children. This message encourages them to strive to accept responsibility and is, therefore, particularly profound and useful, when our children make major mistakes. It is in those times that they are more apt to withhold information or lie to protect themselves from disciplinary consequences. Therefore, it is most appropriate to remind them that if they did it, they should own it.

How do I use the message – if you're brave enough to do it, be brave enough to own it?

As with all of our messages, our ability to be effective lies in our commitment to discuss our motives for these lessons and our expectations for our child's behavior. As such, it is important to accompany this message with our intention to build honesty, responsibility, and integrity by encouraging our child to own their actions and eventually make better choices, which will lead them toward building healthier, happier lives. In each situation, depending on the gravity of the transgression, we may choose to punish the negative behavior. At the same time, we can praise our child's honesty and ownership of their actions. Sometimes it is the good that comes out of the bad situations that is most profound.

The following example demonstrates how to use accountability to build integrity in a young child.

Example Scenario

Example situation.
6 year old who said a curse word on the school bus.

Example reaction-interaction.
Parent: How was your day?

Child: Um, okay.

Parent: Just okay?

Child: Yeah.

Parent: Something happened?

Child. Yes, I got in trouble today.

Parent: You did?

Child: Yes.

Parent: Tell me about it.

Child: I don't really want to.

Parent: How come?

Child: Because you will be mad and maybe disappointed in me.

Parent: Well, you know what I think: If you are brave enough to do, be brave enough to own it!

Child: I know.

Parent: So, tell me what happened.

Child: Okay. I said a curse word on the bus this morning. And, Ms. Greene corrected me and told Principal Stevens. So, I had to go to the office and sit at recess.

Parent: What happened when Principal Stevens asked you about what you did?

Child: I told her what happened.

Parent: What did happen?

Child: We were riding the bus and another student dared me to say a curse word. So, I did.

Parent: Really? You chose to get in trouble for a dare?

Child: Yes.

Parent: Okay. I assume you know better than to curse on the bus.

Child: Yes.

Parent: So, tell me what you should have done instead.

Child: I should have said, no, or ignored him.

Parent: Yes. How did it feel to lose your recess?

Child: Not good. All my friends were playing ball and I really wanted to play, too.

Parent: So, did you learn something from this?

Child: Yes, don't curse on the bus.

Parent: Good. There's one more thing I need to tell you.

Child: What? Are you going to punish me, too?

Parent: No. It sounds like Principal Stevens did that already.

Child: Yes.

Parent: I want to tell you that I'm proud of you.

Child: Really? Why?

Parent: Yes. It is important to me that you owned your actions when Principal Stevens asked you about it. And, then again with me. Now, you will have to tell your dad tonight, too. But, I am proud of you for owning your mistakes and learning from them.

Child: Thanks, Mom.

Discussion is key to building the parent-child relationship and correcting poor behaviors. All children engage in naughty acts at times. Yet, the child who takes ownership of their actions is more likely to readily volunteer information about themselves. For instance, they will tell us when they get in trouble. And, while it is imperative that we address the negative behaviors in order to correct them, it is equally important to point out the positive choices children make in the process. The above example highlights a child that chose to tell the truth to each adult in the situation, owning their behaviors. The act of having to retell the story is a punishment in and of itself, coupled with the punishment doled out at school. And, therefore, there may not be a need to punish again but there is a need to praise the good behavior so if ever the child misbehaves again (and they will), they will be more likely to continue to own their transgressions.

EVALUATION

As a parent, why do I use this message?

I believe that there is an overall lack of ownership over the negative actions and words we put out into the world these days. As a parent who values kindness and positivity, I want my children to think before they act and to spread love not hate. To that end, I believe that if more people were held accountable for their actions or the things they say, they would stop the negative behavior. So, I teach my children that if we are brave enough to engage in a behavior, we need to own it; take responsibility; show our flaws. This helps to build their honesty and responsibility, as I hold them accountable for their actions. Hopefully, this will also help shape them toward a positive persona as they avoid making poor choices.

As a child, what does this message mean to me and how does it make me feel?

If I'm not brave enough to tell you about it, I probably shouldn't do it. I think twice about doing bad things because I don't want to have to own it.

REFLECTION

What do I think about this message?

Take a moment to reflect on using the message, *if you're brave enough to do it, be brave enough to own it.* Ask yourself:
> ➤ Is it relevant for my children?
> ➤ Does it help to build our parent-child relationship?

> ➢ Am I comfortable saying it out loud?
> ➢ Does it reflect a message that I want my children to understand and believe?
> ➢ Does it help me to encourage my children to be happy?
> ➢ Does it help me to alleviate my children's feelings of anxiety or sadness?

What intentional message will I use?

Based on your reflection, consider whether to adopt this message or to modify it for your use. If you chose something different, create your own message by writing it here.

I will build accountability in my children by saying ...

Chapter 16
Responsibility

It's your responsibility to stay close to me.

What is the message?

It's your responsibility to stay close to me.

What is the purpose of the message?

The purpose of the message, it's your responsibility to stay close to me, is to teach personal safety responsibility in our children.

EXPLORATION

What is responsibility in children?

For the purposes of this book, responsibility refers to *the opportunity of our children to make decisions independently*. Parents typically agree that we want to develop independent children. Yet, how do we begin to develop the independent child when they are just learning to navigate the world. One way to do this is by encouraging our children to become responsible, beginning at an early age. As they grow, they begin to exhibit positive qualities associated with responsible children. These characteristics are similar to and connected with the characteristics of the other integrity concepts. For example, responsible children are more likely to engage in appropriate actions by doing what's right, owning their actions, and accepting the consequences of those actions. Therefore, teaching responsibility is interrelated with developing integrity and results in positive emotional, cognitive, and behavioral development within our children.

Why encourage my child to be responsible?

The development of responsibility allows children to explore the concepts of independence and control. While we tend to focus more on independence, control is often overlooked. Yet, this concept is similarly important. Control, or our perceptions of control, is intensely powerful and heavily influences our mental health. For instance, when we believe that we have no control over our lives or our environments, we become perpetually stressed, increasing the likelihood that we develop anxiety and depression. Alternatively, when we perceive we have some control over our lives and our environments, we are able to maintain healthier levels of stress, avoiding negative outcomes and maintaining our mental health. Therefore, to help our children gain a sense of control over their lives, we can teach them to be responsible. And, we can do so using intentional messaging.

How do I develop responsible children?

Parents can identify an area they deem important and use it to develop responsibility. One area we can use to encourage responsible children and the one selected for this book, is personal safety. When initiating the independent child through responsibility, we can address the critical matter of safety while simultaneously addressing the skill development. Within safety, we may choose to focus on safe interactions with other people or safety within the environment. For example, as is the case within this book, we can teach our children to stay close to us when we are outside of the home such as in the grocery store, at the park, or at an event; thus encouraging their independence in the task (while keeping an eye on them) and demonstrating that they can protect themselves in their environment. Choosing safety as a focus for developing responsibility early on allows us to scaffold our safety lessons as they age and develop, whereby we may choose to focus on the environment initially then migrate to teaching safety with others, or vice versa.

What if I don't want to start with safety – are there other areas that I can initiate the development of responsibility in my child?

Another area we can use to develop responsibility in our children is to focus on their physical space. For instance, if we value a clean house, we can encourage our children to be responsible for cleaning up their toys. This encourages their independence in the task and demonstrates that they can control the quality of their environment. As we are beginning this process early on, it is imperative that we select an area that we believe is important for them to grasp early on. Thus, we should contemplate and intentionally select the area we believe will be most appropriate for developing responsibility in our children initially. Then, we incorporate additional lessons as they age and develop.

IMPLEMENTATION

When do I tell my children, it's your responsibility to stay close to me?

Using this specific message to build responsibility, we can present it to our children anytime we go outside of the home. For instance, when we go to the grocery store, a movie, the park, or the zoo, we can remind our children that it is there responsibility to stay close to us. Additionally, a prime time to remind them is when we are walking to and from our vehicles, in a parking lot or near a street. We, of course, must also keep an eye on them to keep them safe. But, instilling in them the lessons of personal protection, gives them added control over their environmental safety. If we choose another area to develop, such as the clean house example, then we use it during the times that correlate with the lesson, such as when our child's room is messy and needs to be tidied up.

How do I use the message – it's your responsibility to stay close to me?

The effectiveness of this message hinges on our ability to deliver it in a consistent manner and explain the importance of safety to our children. Therefore, we can begin with an explanation about environmental safety concerns, such as child abduction, accidental mishaps with vehicles, and the scariness for all if separation occurs – whichever is appropriate in the given situation that we are delivering the message. When explaining about safety issues, it is important to give facts in an age appropriate manner and demonstrate the gravity of the situation without causing extreme alarm. It is also important that we explain that children can control some aspects of their environment by being cautious, observant, and responsible. This helps them to get into the habits of safety.

This message does require substantial reminders. Additionally, when our children do fail to stay close to us, we prompt them through questioning. For example, in this case, if we ask them, "What is your responsibility?" They should answer, "To stay close to you!" On the flip side, if our children are conscientious and remain close to us, then we praise their choices and behavior to encourage them to repeat it in the future.

The following example shows how to encourage personal safety, through responsibility.

Example Scenario

Example situation.
A trip to the grocery store with a 3 year old.

Example reaction-interaction.
Parent: We are going run some errands today.
Child: Okay.
Parent: It is very important when we go out and about that you stay close to me. When we are in the parking lot, you have to stay close so that you don't get hurt by the cars driving around. They may not see you. So being close to me is much safer. Don't you think it would hurt if one of them hit you?
Child: Yes.
Parent: Yes, it would. And, when we are in the store, you have to stay close so that we don't get separated from each other. It would scare me if that happened because I would worry that I couldn't find you. Would you be scared, too, if we were separated and you didn't know where I was?

Child: Yes.

Parent: I thought so. See, it would scare us both. So, when we get out of the car and shop in the store, it's your responsibility to stay close to me.

Child: Okay.

Parent: We are both responsible for your safety. I keep an eye on you and protect you. You are careful and make the choice to stay close to me. When you do that, you are choosing to be safe. Does that make sense to you?

Child: Yes.

Parent: What is your responsibility?

Child: To stay close to you.

Parent: Why?

Child: So I don't get hurt or scared. And, I stay safe.

Parent: Exactly! Great job of listening.

Child. Thanks.

Parent: Now, let's go shop.

Explaining the situation ahead of time allows our children to understand our expectations and ask questions if they have them. By putting some responsibility onto our children for their safety, we allow them to have some control in their environmental safety. By delivering the reasons why we want them to stay close to us, they come to understand the rationale behind our directives which in this case is their safety. Through continued discussions, we build the parent-child relationship and teach our children ways to protect themselves, beginning the process at a young age.

EVALUATION

As a parent, why do I use this message?

I want to build responsibility early on in my children to help them gain some independence and feel a sense of control over their lives. Therefore, I chose to do so with their safety. By teaching them ways to protect themselves in their environment and their responsibility to stay close to me, I believe they learn that they play a role in their safety in order to learn to make choices to protect themselves from the dangers of the world. It starts with the dangers associated with moving cars and strangers in the grocery store, but the lessons broaden to other areas of their lives as they age.

As a child, what does this message mean to me and how does it make me feel?

It means that you are trying to keep me safe by teaching me how to protect myself.

REFLECTION

What do I think about this message?

Take a moment to reflect on using the message, *it's your responsibility to stay close to me.* Ask yourself:
> - Is it relevant for my children?
> - Does it help to build our parent-child relationship?
> - Am I comfortable saying it out loud?
> - Does it reflect a message that I want my children to understand and believe?

> ➤ Does it help me to encourage my children to be happy?
> ➤ Does it help me to alleviate my children's feelings of anxiety or sadness?

What intentional message will I use?

Based on your reflection, consider whether to adopt this message or to modify it for your use. If you chose something different, create your own message by writing it here.

I will build responsibility in my children by saying …

Discussion ~ Integrity

Building integrity in our children is a gift that provides them with the foundation to build a life of honor and truth. We do so by encouraging honesty, responsibility, accountability, ownership, and quality decision making. In turn, the virtuous child will be confident, happy, and steadfast in their belief in doing the right thing for themselves and those around them. They will be generous and kind, sharing their positivity with those around them and spreading more honor in our society.

Additionally, as a result of the positive qualities they possess, children with integrity live a life of health and happiness. Furthermore, raising virtuous children brings an added benefit -- parental rewards such as pride, trust, and inspiration because, our children will remind us, as parents, to stay true to our own virtues along the way. In the end, the reciprocity and contagion of integrity makes our children, ourselves and the world around us better.

Part 5 ~ Resilience

Intentional Messages That Develop Resilience

Intentional Messages That Develop Resilience

Resilience – the capacity to recover quickly from difficulties; toughness (Oxford Living Dictionaries)

What is resilience in children?

Resilience in children, in its simplest form, is their *ability to bounce back from setbacks*. Resilient children are able to recover from challenges, adapt to new environments or situations, and plow forward through difficult circumstances, all while maintaining a positive outlook on the future, typically using hope as a precursor to survival. Often times, we recognize that young children are more resilient than adults. That is because they have not been repeatedly knocked down by life struggles. But, after a serious of repeated setbacks or persistent difficult circumstances, they are equally at risk for giving up or developing anxiety or depression as a result. Therefore, it is important to prepare our children for life's challenges by providing them with coping strategies to remain resilient while attaining and/or maintaining health and happiness.

How do I develop resilience in my children?

The entirety of this book focuses on concepts that are proven necessary to produce resilience, such as optimism, self-efficacy, self-belief, belonging, lifelong learning, critical thinking, persistence, and gratitude. For instance, a child who is loved, confident, happy, and virtuous will naturally be able to endure life easier than one who is not. Therefore, it is fitting that the book culminates in exploring resilience and the added concepts in this section, since each principle explored contributes to the development of resilient children.

To help our children develop into resilient adults, parents must primarily focus on lessons that teach our children how to cope. Our children will be faced with many challenges in life, whether by their own creation or by circumstances beyond their control. They must be able to manage each situation in order to persist in spite of the level of difficulty. Therefore, coping skill development is necessary for our children to prevail. The intentional messaging parenting strategy is designed for that purpose. It provides our children with foundational principles that are easily adopted and adapted in order for parents to provide our children with a framework on how to cope with life.

Why develop resilience using intentional messaging?

The world can be a rough and bleak place, surrounded by negativity, causing persistent, personal stress. We may make decisions or take risks and anticipate positive outcomes that instead result in stressful, negative outcomes – divorce, job loss, bankruptcy. Or, we may make all the right choices, yet, still face circumstances beyond our control that test us and cause severe stress – natural disasters, illness, death. Either way, we cannot escape adversities. However, it is our response to those difficulties that define us – whether we allow it to defeat us or whether we fight through it. Therefore, it is our reaction to adversity that show us what we are made of. The same is true for our children. They will face challenges. It is inevitable. Yet, giving them repeated, deliberate messages that encourage them to develop self-motivation through encouragement and positive self-talk will help them to overcome and persist through hardships (cope) instead of giving up. In addition to the previous messages, we can use intentional messages that encourage learning, problem solving, persistence and gratitude to develop resilient children.

Let's explore the resilience messages that help our children to never give up.

Chapter 17
Lifelong Learning

You aren't supposed to know. That's why we learn.

What is the message?

You aren't supposed to know. That's why we learn.

What is the purpose of the message?

The purpose of the message, you aren't supposed to know, that's why we learn, is to encourage our children to develop an appreciation for lifelong learning.

EXPLORATION

What is lifelong learning?

We incorrectly assume that children innately know how to learn, yet research shows that learning is often misunderstood and that our assumptions about how to learn successfully are typically mistaken (Brown et al., 2014). Learning has been examined intensely over the past few years, uncovering many monumental insights. When examining all of these insights, we can assert that learning requires a specific mindset and skillset that focuses on growth, effort, and strategies (Dweck, 2006; Brown et al., 2014; McGuire, 2015; Brocato et al., 2018). Therefore, it is imperative that we teach our children that learning does not occur naturally. Instead, it is an ongoing process that requires deliberate focus and commitment, resulting in the appreciation for and engagement in lifelong learning. Children who embrace lifelong learning in this manner will explore the world, aspire for continued growth, persist toward their goals, and understand that learning never ceases.

Why encourage my child to adopt lifelong learning?

When we encourage our children to recognize and value learning as a lifelong process, it frees them from the ill effects of perfectionism, such as depression and anxiety, and allows them to move on from their mistakes (increasing resilience). In fact, it helps them to view mistakes as a gift, examine their role in each given situation, and look for the lessons in each experience because each experience is worth learning from. This, in turn, encourages our child's growth and their commitment to do better the next time they are presented with a similar situation. Our child's ability to learn from their mistakes relies on their ability to engage in reflection, *the act of giving serious thought or consideration* to a situation. Reflection leads to higher achievement and produces more successful life outcomes, including health and happiness because it encourages continued growth. Therefore, lifelong learning contributes to resilience and overall health.

How do I encourage my children to learn?

In order to help our children learn, parents should present learning as a process. First, we explain to our children that they aren't supposed to know things without first learning them. For some reason, our children assume they should know everything before being taught. For example, children may think they should know all of their multiplication facts after their first lesson. The outcome of this misconception is frustration, leading to anger or sadness. Therefore, encouraging learning requires us to teach children to have patience and view learning as a long-term, ongoing process.

Next, parents should explain that learning can be enhanced through effort. We do so by encouraging our children to adopt what's known as a growth mindset, whereby we believe that intelligence can be developed through effort (Dweck, 2006). We explain to our children that our brains grow and strengthen with learning, which expands our intelligence and, as a result, increases our successes. In the end, our effort is the most important component of learning; therefore, we reward our children's efforts to learn in order to increase their commitment to it. By simply encouraging them to commit to do their best when learning and praising them for it, we reinforce that their effort is paramount.

Why do I need to address learning – isn't that what school is for?

While the education system contributes to student learning, parents play a crucial role in either encouraging or discouraging learning as a process. In order to encourage it, we must avoid presenting learning in a negative manner. Many parents fall into the unintentional trap associated with presenting learning in negative light. We primarily do so through our approach to homework. It is no surprise that many parents are reticent to reengage in homework with our young children. However, when we present negative feelings regarding homework to our children through avoidance or discouragement, they quickly adopt those views, setting homework up to be a challenging ordeal for everyone in the household. Thus, in recent years, homework has contributed to the breakdown of many parent-child relationships.

We must never underestimate our power to set our children up for success or failure through our own beliefs, words, actions, and feelings. Because of this, we play the primary role in learning for our children and should not avoid or discourage it, intentionally or not. Instead, we should present it positively, even adopting lifelong learning for ourselves. If we endorse homework as an opportunity for our children to showcase their learning and/or for us to give them needed assistance and support, we make learning fun and engaging. This shifts homework from an unfavorable experience to a favorable one. Additionally, when we experience learning together with our children, we create another opportunity to strengthen our parent-child relationship.

IMPLEMENTATION

When do I tell my children, you aren't supposed to know, that's why we learn?

The opportunities for learning are endless; therefore, the opportunities to encourage learning are endless, too. We can easily encourage learning of a sport, hobby, or interest that our child gravitates toward as a way to do so in a positive manner. However, most parents will naturally piggyback on our child's education when encouraging them to approach learning as an ongoing, positive process. This message, in particular, centers on helping a child to understand that they aren't wired to innately know everything. Learning takes time, effort, practice, and patience.

How do I use the message – you aren't supposed to know, that's why we learn?

This particular message focuses on how we can alleviate our child's anxieties for not knowing everything or their misconception that learning should be easy. Our best learning occurs through our struggles with difficult material or tasks. For example, learning to ride a bike is one of the most arduous and intense tasks to accomplish. It requires all of our body systems working simultaneously to defeat gravity. Yet, once we get it, we don't ever forget it. That's lasting learning. Therefore, we diffuse meltdowns by pointing out that they shouldn't know the material or how to complete a task. By doing this, we are giving them permission to engage in the learning process, without damaging their self-concept about their intelligence or their capabilities. We shift the focus from the negative feelings of frustration or avoidance, to the positive opportunity to learn and accomplish.

The following example demonstrates how to encourage a child to appreciate learning.

Example Scenario

Example situation.
A 5 year old learning to subtract.

Example reaction-interaction.
Parent: It's time for your homework. What do you have tonight?
Child: I have math.

Parent: What are you learning in math right now?

Child: Subtraction.

Parent: What do you think about it?

Child: It's hard and I don't understand it.

Parent: Subtraction can be challenging when we first try to learn it.

Child: I just can't do it.

Parent: Why do you say that?

Child: Some of my friends got it right away in class but I still mess up.

Parent: How do you feel about that?

Child: Bad.

Parent: I get that. Let me share some facts about learning with you. I think it may help you to feel better.

Child: Okay.

Parent: First off, we don't all learn the same way. So, your classmates will get some things quickly and you may not. Other things, you will get quickly and they may not. So, learning is unique to us and what matters is that we stay focused on ourselves.

Child: Okay.

Parent: Second, learning is fun. If we figure out how to make it fun for you, you will enjoy it and it will come quicker.

Child: Really?

Parent. Yes. Third, learning is exercise for our brains. When we learn, our brains get stronger and that helps us to get smarter. So, no matter how hard subtraction may be, if you stick with it, you can and will learn it.

Child: Cool.

Parent: You aren't supposed to know how to do subtraction. That's why we learn. You are going to make mistakes. But every mistake helps you to learn. Sometimes we even learn better because we mess up.

Child: Really?

Parent. Yes. And, homework is super cool. You know why?

Child: No! Why?
Parent: Homework is a time for us to learn together. You can share your learning with me and we can practice together. I can even help you learn more. So, it makes the time special.
Child: Okay.
Parent: How do you feel now that you know more about learning?
Child: Better. Thanks.
Parent: Great! Are you ready to show me what you know and then learn how to subtract?
Child: Yes!

When our children struggle to understand concepts quickly, they often get frustrated. This becomes exacerbated if their classmates are grasping the concepts quicker. This may result in our children developing anxiety to learn. Therefore, it is important to discuss that we all learn differently, that learning can be fun, that it makes our brains stronger, that they will make mistakes, and that they really aren't supposed to know everything because then what would be the use of school. Discussions about their feelings and experiences allows us to better understand them and allows them to gain the support they need for learning success.

EVALUATION

As a parent, why do I use this message?

Learning is an important emphasis in parenting my children. I want them to view life as an opportunity to grow and develop continuously. Through a love of learning and a commitment to learning over a lifetime, their opportunities are endless. They can accomplish whatever they want to as long as they understand that through effort and commitment they can learn anything. Additionally, lifelong learning alleviates the pressures of perfectionism and encourages self-reflection, both of which I view as helpful for persisting through life, regardless of the challenges they may face. In short, I view lifelong learning as the impetus for my children's success.

As a child, what does this message mean to me and how does it make me feel?

It means to me that even though I want to get things right on my first try, I don't have to because I am just learning it. There are things that I shouldn't know yet. It also reminds me that I need to learn more.

REFLECTION

What do I think about this message?

Take a moment to reflect on using the message, *you aren't supposed to know; that's why we learn.* Ask yourself:
- Is it relevant for my children?
- Does it help to build our parent-child relationship?
- Am I comfortable saying it out loud?
- Does it reflect a message that I want my children to understand and believe?
- Does it help me to encourage my children to be happy?
- Does it help me to alleviate my children's feelings of anxiety or sadness?

158

What intentional message will I use?

Based on your reflection, consider whether to adopt this message or to modify it for your use. If you chose something different, create your own message by writing it here.

I will develop learning in my children by saying ...

Chapter 18
Problem Solving

There's always a solution.

What is the message?

There's always a solution.

What is the purpose of the message?

The purpose of the message, there's always a solution, is to encourage the development of problem solving and critical thinking skills in our children.

EXPLORATION

What is problem solving?

As with making good decisions, successful problem solving is a process that requires specific skill development. Children who develop this skill are able to consider all sides of a problem, the impacts of various solutions, and weigh the risks and benefits of each action in order to make the best decision with the information they have. Successful problem solvers are able to think critically about situations, gather information to make informed decisions, and ask for assistance, when needed. Those who become comfortable in problem solving will often offer solutions to various situations and are comfortable and confident in their abilities. They realize that there is not just one way to address a challenge but numerous options, including the option to do nothing. This realization aids the critical thinking process and leads to the development of their abilities to analytically assess situations later in life.

Why help my child to develop problem solving skills?

When we encourage the development of problem solving skills in our children, we will immediately see the benefits when our children offer us solutions to various problems. Sometimes, this comes with both pride and annoyance as they can make good arguments for how and why they should get their way. Still, the benefits outweigh the nuisance as it shows initiative and complex cognitive functioning when our children engage in the problem solving process. The more they do it, the better they become. This helps them to gain independence and confidence in themselves. It also allows us to gain confidence in their abilities to function independently, too. Therefore, when we encourage problem solving and critical thinking, we know that our children will have the tools necessary to successfully function as an adult. As a result, our children will develop resilience, as challenges will not stifle them. They will be able to progress through the hardships of life, by finding appropriate solutions to their problems and addressing them head on. In the end, their abilities to problem solve will help them attain and/or maintain their health and happiness as they will believe in their abilities to work through their hardships.

How do I teach my child to solve problems?

Teaching the steps associated with a standard, problem solving process at an early age helps our children to develop problem solving skills (Morin, 2019). First, pinpoint and examine the problem. Initially, we may need to model for our children how to do this. But, as they practice the process, we encourage them to identify the problem. If they get stuck, we ask questions to help them explore their feelings and state the problem in their own words. Second, find two potential courses of action to remedy the problem. As they get older, we allow them to identify two possible options, then increase the number of potential options to progress the complexity of the process. Third, explore the possible outcomes of each choice, both risks and benefits. Again, once we model how to do this, we can migrate toward allowing them to do so with less guidance. Next, select a solution. We encourage them to choose the best option then implement it to solve the problem. We can remind them that if the solution selected doesn't work, they can consider the other solution discussed or come up with new alternatives. Last, reflect on the process and outcomes. This step is sometimes overlooked but it is necessary in order to determine what is learned from the situation. Therefore, it is important to gain their feedback via reflection regarding the outcome of their actions. Did they satisfactorily solve the problem? How did they feel about the process and resolution? Reflection helps them to think about the entirety of the process, identify difficulties and strengths they experienced, and examine what they learned about themselves and the situation. It helps them to learn from each experience in order to apply those lessons to future situations. As they become more proficient with the problem solving process, we allow them to complete the steps, providing minimal or no assistance. In the end, our children may master the process but still require our guidance, wisdom or advice as they grow and their problems grow, too.

IMPLEMENTATION

When do I tell my children, there's always a solution?

There are many instances where we can offer to our children that there's always a solution. Whether they are looking for a missing toy, attempting to complete schoolwork, or trying to decide what to put on their birthday list, we can encourage them to use the problem solving process to come to a resolution and decision. We start with small issues, then we encourage them to come up with solutions to more challenging situations. No matter the situation, we use facilitated discussion with our children to model then assist them in the development of these skills. We encourage them to reflect on their decisions to learn more from the experience and adjust for future challenges.

How do I use the message – there's always a solution?

Using this specific message to develop problem solving skills, indicates to our children that we rarely have to settle for the situation that life presents us. There is always something we can do to address our situations; even if what we must do is accept the situation as our reality, which then typically requires a mindset change. Therefore, we can use this message anytime we are faced with a problem that is age appropriate for their understanding. We can first model the process by going through steps aloud for our children to witness. Then, we allow them to go through the process themselves, using their own problems. As they become more skilled problem solvers, the process becomes quicker and easier for our children, oftentimes happening in their minds without requiring discussion. During those times, they only require our assistance when they get stuck in the process. The best approach to helping them get past any snags in the process is to ask questions so that they can continue to think critically about the problem until they come to the resolution of their choice.

The following example demonstrates how to walk a child through the problem solving process.

Example Scenario

Example situation.
3 year old who can't find a toy.

Example reaction-interaction.
Child: Mom!
Parent: What is it? You seem upset.
Child: Yes. I can't find my bear!
Parent: Hmm. That is making you sad?
Child: Yes.
Parent: Okay. So, your problem is that you can't find your bear.
Child: Yes.
Parent: How do you think you can find it? Give me two ways.
Child: Look for it.
Parent: That's one. Or?
Child: I don't know.
Parent: What about if you think really hard about the last time you had it? Maybe you would remember where it is?
Child: Yes.
Parent: Okay, you can either go look for it or think about where you were when you had it last. Tell me what would happen if you go look for it.
Child: I could find it.
Parent: You could go look and find it. What if you don't find it?
Child: Then, it is still lost.

Parent: Yes. Now, what if you thought hard about where you were last time you had your bear. What could happen then?

Child: I could remember.

Parent: Yes, you may remember. What if you don't remember?

Child: Then, it is still lost.

Parent: True. Which do you think is the better solution? Should you look first or try to remember first? Because you can do both. You just have to think about which order to do them in. Try one then the other, maybe?

Child: Yes. What if I think about it first, then go look.

Parent: That sounds like a great plan. Now, think really hard. When was the last time you had your bear?

Child: Before lunch.

Parent: Okay. So, I called you to come to lunch. What did you do with your bear?

Child: I don't know.

Parent: Did you leave it in your room? Or did you bring it into the kitchen with you?

Child: Oh! I brought it into the kitchen!

Parent: What did you do then?

Child: I put it down to eat!

Parent: Where should you go look for your bear?

Child: In the kitchen! I'm going look.

Parent: *Silence.*

Child: I found it!! I found my bear!!

Parent: Great. So, what did you do to find your bear?

Child: I thought about where I had him last and went to look there.

Parent: You sure did and that worked out for you. How are you feeling now that you solved your problem?

Child: Great!

As we can see, it takes much more time and discussion to walk a young child through the problem solving process than it does to simply tell the child the answer. All along the parent knew the bear was in the kitchen. Yet, we don't tell them because then there is no lesson in that. These types of scenarios early on, expose them to the process in order for them to get comfortable with doing it on their own. Next time bear goes missing, chances are, the child will know at least two approaches to attempt to find it. That may not prevent them from asking us to do it. But, we will both know that they are capable of the task.

EVALUATION

As a parent, why do I use this message?

I'm always happily impressed when my children voluntarily offer solutions to problems or present options for addressing an issue. I know they will make mistakes, they will get frustrated, maybe even angry, but because they know how to come up with solutions, they will be at an advantage later in life. I want to set them up to function independently and know that regardless of the situation, there is always a solution. I also want them to consider the consequences of their choices. I believe that this will allow them to look at life more positively and feel more in control of their lives, resulting in them being more resilient.

As a child, what does this message mean to me and how does it make me feel?

It means that there is more than one solution to a problem, if you just keep trying you will be able to figure it out on your own. If not, I can always ask for help but there is always a way to work things out.

REFLECTION

What do I think about this message?

Take a moment to reflect on using the message, *there's always a solution.* Ask yourself:

> ➢ Is it relevant for my children?
> ➢ Does it help to build our parent-child relationship?
> ➢ Am I comfortable saying it out loud?
> ➢ Does it reflect a message that I want my children to understand and believe?
> ➢ Does it help me to encourage my children to be happy?
> ➢ Does it help me to alleviate my children's feelings of anxiety or sadness?

What intentional message will I use?

Based on your reflection, consider whether to adopt this message or to modify it for your use. If you chose something different, create your own message by writing it here.

I will develop problem solving skills in my children by saying ...

Chapter 19
Persistence

Don't give up!

What is the message?

Don't give up!

What is the purpose of the message?

The purpose of the message, don't give up, is to encourage our children to endure and persist in spite of challenges in order to accomplish goals.

EXPLORATION

What is persistence in children?

For the purposes of this book, persistence in children refers to their *continued engagement in a course of action in spite of difficulty or opposition.* When we are confronted by challenges, obstacles, or resistance in life, some of us endure; while others give up. The difference in these approaches relies solely on our choice to persist. Persistence is a necessary quality for people to learn something difficult, attain long-term goals, and stick to commitments, including relationships and life, in general. Therefore, those who choose to persist in spite of challenges are more likely to attain success. The same is true of our children. Children who choose persistence will focus on the positives of situations and learn from any mistakes in order to adjust their approach when faced with challenges. Children who adopt a mindset of sustained persistence will acknowledge their negative feelings then use them as motivation to keep going. We typically view these children as strong, particularly in their mental capacity. And, when they gain the rewards of achievement, persistent children will be encouraged to continue to endure throughout their lives.

Why encourage my child to persist through challenges?

Persistence, coupled with passion, contributes to our child's ability to develop grit for long term achievement and success (Duckworth, 2016). As parents, we teach our children persistence so that they are able to accomplish goals, strive for healthy, reciprocal relationships, and ultimately, endure life's challenges without falling into negative traps that lead to a disconnect with life. Those traps include the development of negative coping habits, such as drug use, which oftentimes results from our inability to deal with life pressures. Some, given very good reasons, feel the need to escape life. Yet, others choose to use these negative situations as motivators to push through to attain more positivity in their lives. They view life as a cycle of good and bad times, understanding that they have control over certain areas of their lives and accepting the challenge to persist until they are the victors. As parents, we want to set our children up for success and help them to develop positive coping strategies in spite of difficulties. Therefore, encouraging them to not give up is a way to motivate our children toward accomplishing their goals, serving as another tool that develops resilience.

How much pressure should I put on my children to persist?

Parents must be delicate and careful with the pressure we place on children. While we want to push them to accomplish goals, we must pick and choose which areas of our child's lives require our encouragement for them to keep going and which areas are okay to let go. For instance, if our child is exploring playing baseball for the first time, we can encourage them to commit to and finish out the season; but, we may also recognize that if there is no interest in the sport, then they may not want to play again next season. Making them play in spite of their lack of interest can backfire on us and in turn, negatively impact their mindset toward persistence and negatively impact our parent-child relationship. Therefore, we should encourage our children to not give up on areas we deem most important in their lives, such as their education, or to keep going when things get difficult when they are trying to accomplish a long-term goal that is important to them.

Does persistence always produce positive outcomes?

Persistence is required to accomplish long-term and/or difficult goals, but persistence in negative situations is more of a detriment than a benefit. For instance, when we endure an unhealthy or harmful relationship, we are technically persisting through a difficult situation yet the outcomes are a detriment to our health and happiness. Therefore, it is imperative that we teach our children how to evaluate their goals, relationships, and commitments to ensure that they are good for them through reflection. This will allow them to determine whether or not they are engaged in positive, healthy lifestyles, conducive to creating meaningful lives. While endurance can progress us to be successful, endurance applied to bad situations can keep us down, resulting in the opposite outcome of our intentions. In those times, it is important for our children to learn how to deal with failure and move on. This allows them to leave a negative circumstance while simultaneously persisting through life.

IMPLEMENTATION

When do I tell my children, don't give up?

We encourage our children to stay the course when they are attempting new tasks, working toward a valued goal, or frustrated by a setback in their course of action. Whether they are trying to swim 10 laps in the pool instead of 5 or they are struggling to learn long division, we can encourage them to not give up because their persistence will allow them to attain their goal. Therefore, we use this message as a motivator to give our children the extra push to overcome challenges, attain goals, or pursue their dreams.

How do I use the message – don't give up?

The effectiveness of this message hinges on our ability to encourage our children to push through without putting excessive pressure on them to do so. Some pressure in the form of encouragement can help; too much pressure that teeters on reprimand can hinder. Therefore, parents must be mindful of how their children will respond to the message and make certain to engage in facilitated discussion so that our children understand that our message is grounded in encouragement to develop persistence.

The following example highlights an instance to encourage persistence in our children.

Example Scenario

Example situation.
6 year old learning how to tie shoes.

Example reaction-interaction.
Child: Mom, I just can't do this! I can't tie my shoes!

Parent: Is there something I can help you with?

Child: You can tie my shoes for me.

Parent: I could do that but how would you learn. I can teach you how to do it and then you need to practice.

Child: Ugh.

Parent: Tell me how you are feeling.

Child: Frustrated!

Parent: I hear that and understand that when we learn something challenging that it can get frustrating. Take a deep breath and count to 10.

Child: *Breathes. Counts...*

Parent: Okay. Now tell me what you know about tying your shoes.

Child: I know to cross and pull. Then make ears, cross again; but I keep losing my grip and dropping the strings. Then it comes out like this.

Parent: Don't give up. You can take breaks here and there when you get frustrated. But, you can either allow this to aggravate you or you can keep at it until you get it. If you quit, you will be sad in the long run. If you stay with it, you will feel so happy when you do get it. You may not get it today or tomorrow, but at some point, you will learn. So, don't give up! Do you understand?

Child: Yes. It is just so hard.

Parent: I know. How about I show you how to do it one more time and then you try again?

Child: Okay.

Through discussion, we encourage a sharing of thoughts and feelings in order to help our children accomplish a challenging task or goal. There will be many times where they are frustrated by a situation or feel as if they can't do something. It is in those times that they need our encouragement to stay committed to the task until they complete and/or achieve it.

EVALUATION

As a parent, why do I use this message?

It is important that my children understand that life is not always easy, even when we make good decisions. The most rewarding things in life are difficult to attain, which makes them even more meaningful. I want my children to realize their goals and dreams by putting forth the effort, time, and practice. They must stay in the struggle in order to attain their goals. I believe that my respectful encouragement is helpful as a motivator until they figure out how to self-motivate to persist without me.

As a child, what does this message mean to me and how does it make me feel?

It means that I should try until I get something even though it is hard. It makes me feel like you are encouraging me to keep going. And, when I hear it, I don't want to give up. I want to keep going.

REFLECTION

What do I think about this message?

Take a moment to reflect on using the message, *don't give up*. Ask yourself:

> ➤ Is it relevant for my children?
> ➤ Does it help to build our parent-child relationship?
> ➤ Am I comfortable saying it out loud?
> ➤ Does it reflect a message that I want my children to understand and believe?
> ➤ Does it help me to encourage my children to be happy?
> ➤ Does it help me to alleviate my children's feelings of anxiety or sadness?

What intentional message will I use?

Based on your reflection, consider whether to adopt this message or to modify it for your use. If you chose something different, create your own message by writing it here.

I will develop persistence in my children by saying ...

Chapter 20
Gratitude

Thank you!

What is the message?

Thank you!

What is the purpose of the message?

The purpose of the message, thank you, is to raise thoughtful children who practice gratitude.

EXPLORATION

What is gratitude in children?

Gratitude is the mindful practice of *being thankful* and *showing appreciation via kindness*. When we practice gratitude, we are engaged in ourselves and our environment, assessing our feelings, examining our roles, and deciphering how we impact others and how they impact us. Gratitude is an example of mindfulness in practice. We must be present and connected to our lives to recognize that with which we are grateful for and then choose to demonstrate our appreciation for those gifts. Gratitude, therefore, pushes us all toward positivity. Consequentially, children who practice gratitude are connected to their lives, their relationships, and their environments. They recognize the rewards in their lives and choose to acknowledge them, resulting in children who are generous, kind, and thoughtful. This produces infectious children that people want to be around as they spread respect, thoughtfulness, and positivity to the world around them.

Why encourage my child to practice gratitude?

Recent research examining gratitude has shown that it has tremendous benefits, making it a focus for development and practice. Practicing gratitude has a direct, positive impact on the outcome of resilience. Furthermore, the practice of intentional gratitude increases our child's ability to focus on the present, assess their feelings, and determine how the world impacts them. It allows them to respond to the world in a positive manner in spite of the difficulties they encounter. Additionally, according to a recent study, "gratitude has the power to heal, energize, and transform lives by enhancing people psychologically, spiritually, physically, and cognitively" (Wilson, 2016). Therefore, when we encourage our children to be grateful and demonstrate appreciation, we are providing them with another valuable coping strategy to create meaningful lives in a healthy and happy manner.

Are there other benefits of gratitude?

Gratitude is acutely interconnected to the principles previously discussed including but not limited to positivity, kindness, awareness, self-efficacy, learning, and persistence. Gratitude fosters optimism. It promotes compassion and a respect for others. It requires attentiveness and self-reflection. It increases student learning and success (Wilson, 2016). And, it allow us to appreciate life when it is stellar and persist through life when it is tough. Therefore, of all the lessons, gratitude is the easiest to implement, yet requires a culmination of all the lessons into one act, making it the most compelling.

How do I develop grateful children?

We teach our children gratitude through the simple act of modeling it to them. By verbalizing why we are thankful, we can show our children how to practice gratitude themselves. We begin by using the intentional message of thank you in order to show appreciation to our children when they are kind or do something meaningful. We also encourage them to say thank you to others who demonstrate thoughtfulness. As our children grow, we encourage them to practice gratitude through other methods in order to advance their skill. For instance, our children can complete activities such as creating a gratitude journal, writing gratitude letters, designing gratitude art, or engaging in gratitude discussions. These activities give them a medium to acknowledge their appreciation for the joys, lessons, and people in their lives. In the end, when we both demonstrate and expect gratitude as a core foundational value, we provide our children with a meaningful coping skill to flourish for life.

IMPLEMENTATION

When do I tell my children, thank you?

We can demonstrate gratitude to our children when they do something kind, considerate, meaningful, or helpful. We can also thank our children when they follow our instructions or commands with ease as to convey to them our appreciation for their listening and following direction, which encourages the behavior to continue. Additionally, we can instruct our children to use gratitude when we, or someone else, show them kindness, courteousness, or help. Furthermore, we can encourage our children to practice gratitude by intentionally identifying all of the blessings in their lives at any time.

How do I use the message – thank you?

The easiest way to implement this message is to, first and foremost, thank our children. If we want them to practice gratitude, we do so ourselves; otherwise, we are asking them to engage in behaviors that we don't, making our message incongruent with our actions. The synergy between our messages and our actions is a must. Therefore, we initiate the development of gratitude in our children by simply thanking them. Additionally, when we thank them, we must also describe the behavior we appreciate and why. This allows them to recognize the behavior that resulted in appreciation and the impact it had on us. Pointing out their positive behaviors through gratitude, in turn, reinforces those positive behaviors making them more likely to occur again in the future. So, by thanking our children, we not only model for them how to practice gratitude, but we also encourage the continuance of their positive behaviors.

The second way to use the message is to remind our children to thank others for their acts of kindness. This again should be accompanied by discussion as to why the behavior warrants acknowledgment. Initially, we may provide the insights to our children. But, as they age, we allow them to tell us why they are showing appreciation to someone else. Over time, this becomes a habit, where they appreciate the actions of others and thank them for it. In doing so, our children are in essence pointing out positive behaviors of friends, family, and strangers alike. Again, simply thanking others has additional positive outcomes because it often continues the positive interactions, contributes to quality relationships and demonstrates a level of respect for humankind.

Another way to use this message is to identify the gifts in our lives and encouraging our children to do the same. This exercise allows us to teach our children how to recognize the positives in life. We encourage them to focus on their fortune through reflection, whereby they identify the benefits, advantages, and blessings in their lives. This produces children who will oftentimes understand that our relationships are the most important part of life.

The following two simple examples encourage our children to practice gratitude.

This example demonstrates how to thank our children for their thoughtfulness.

Example Scenario

Example situation.
4 year old who inquired about parent's ailment.

Example reaction-interaction.
Parent: Good morning.
Child: Good morning.
Parent: How'd you sleep last night?
Child: Good. How about you?
Parent: I slept well, too.
Child: Is your head feeling better?
Parent: Yes, it is. Thank you! You remembered I had a headache before bed?
Child: Yes.
Parent: Well, that it is very thoughtful of you to remember and very considerate of you to ask me about it. I appreciate your concern for me. I'm feeling much better today. Thank you for asking.
Child: You're welcome.

Parent: You know, I'm one lucky mom to have you for my child. I'm thankful that I got you.
Child: I'm happy I got you, too.

As previously recommended, we not only show gratitude but we also explain what behavior we are thankful for and why so that our child can clearly tie the positive action to the positive outcome. The child leaves the situation with pride over their unprompted courtesy. And, the parent reinforced the act of kindness by simply showing gratitude. Additionally, by pointing out that we are thankful to be our child's parent, we show them that they are special to us while we model a simple way to practice gratitude.

This example demonstrates how to encourage our child to show appreciation for someone else's act of kindness.

Example situation.
5 year old who enjoyed a vacation compliments of their grandparents.

Example reaction-interaction.
Child: I love the beach!
Parent: Me too!
Child: It is my happy place!!
Parent: Then, I bet you are glad that Granny and Paw took you to the beach for vacation.
Child: I sure am.
Parent: What do you want to tell Granny and Paw?
Child: Thank you, Granny and Paw!
Parent: For what?
Child: For taking me on a beach vacation.
Parent: Why?
Child: Because the beach makes me happy.

Parent: That's a good start. Now say it all together.

Child: Thank you, Granny and Paw, for taking me on a beach vacation because the beach makes me happy.

Granny and Paw: You're welcome. It makes us happy to go to the beach with you, too.

Parent: It is important to tell others that we appreciate their thoughtfulness when they choose to do something kind for us. We also need to be acknowledge what they did for us and why it matters to us.

Child: Okay.

In this example, we encourage our child to show appreciation for an act of kindness from someone else. In doing so, we encourage them to not only thank others but also state what they are grateful for and why. This helps our children to reflect on the experience to determine how it impacts them as they are practicing gratitude. Additionally, it demonstrates to others respect for their kindness, therefore, promoting those relationships as mutually positive.

EVALUATION

As a parent, why do I use this message?

Gratitude is a simple jester with complex, robust benefits. It encourages mindfulness, self-reflection, awareness, positivity, kindness, and virtue – all lessons that I want my children to embrace – in one act. It also comes with the added benefits of contributing to my child's resilience and success, providing lasting positive outcomes. Therefore, I encourage my children to practice gratitude so that they are courteous, thoughtful people who view others with equal respect and kindness.

Lahna Rung Roche

As a child, what does this message mean to me and how does it make me feel?

It makes me feel happy when you tell me thank you. Saying thank you means you are respecting people and has good consequences, like when I waived at the lady that let us cross the road; she waived back.

REFLECTION

What do I think about this message?

Take a moment to reflect on using the message, thank you! Ask yourself:
> - Is it relevant for my children?
> - Does it help to build our parent-child relationship?
> - Am I comfortable saying it out loud?
> - Does it reflect a message that I want my children to understand and believe?
> - Does it help me to encourage my children to be happy?
> - Does it help me to alleviate my children's feelings of anxiety or sadness?

What intentional message will I use?

Based on your reflection, consider whether to adopt this message or to modify it for your use. If you chose something different, create your own message by writing it here.

I will develop gratitude in my children by saying ...

Discussion ~ Resilience

By developing resilience in our children, we are providing them with a strong foundation to endure the positive and negative experiences of life. We do so by teaching them principles such as lifelong learning, problem solving, persistence, and gratitude in order to develop their character and increase the likelihood that they will bounce back from any setbacks they face in their lifetime. And, we foster reflection to encourage self-awareness and personal growth to strengthen their resolve as reflection directly influences resilience.

Our children will, without a doubt, face obstacles that will make them doubt their ability to persist. Yet, it is particularly important, in those times, that they have the framework and skills necessary to persevere. By using these intentional messages that develop resilience, we provide our children with the strong principles and healthy coping skills required to create a positive self-concept, develop healthy, rewarding relationships, and embrace life as a gift to be valued. Consequentially, by developing resilient children, we give them the greatest opportunity to create a life of health, happiness, and success.

Closing Remarks

There is no singular, correct way to parent. The trick is to find the right way to parent that fits each of us and each of our children. This book aims to provide parents and other caregivers with a new parenting strategy that focuses on intentional messages, coupled with facilitated discussions, to provide our children with deliberate lessons that will serve as a foundation for the development of healthy, happy adults. It is but one tool to incorporate into our parenting arsenal in order to develop our children's emotional, social, academic, and personal wellbeing.

The utilization of respectful, sustained communications with our children is the impetus for success with this method. Dialogue is necessary in order to convey our message, explain the rationale behind the lesson, and clearly state our expectations of our children. Dialogue is also necessary in order to gain our child's insights to understand where they are in their thoughts and feelings. Through respectful discussion, we strengthen our understanding of one another and our relationship as a whole.

The messages provided in this book are grounded in research-based principles that help children to thrive and succeed. These messages may be used as is, adapted to meet the needs of each parent and every child, or replaced by messages better-suited to your family or the needs of your children. When adapting or creating new messages, we must be deliberate in our choice of words and ensure our child's understanding of our lessons (refer to tips in the resource section). One way to verify their understanding is to have our child summarize in their own words what the message means to them. This verification is necessary because we don't want the impact of our message to be something other than what we intend. If our children misinterpret our words, there is a potential for the message to fail or even backfire. Therefore, through continued dialogue and verification, we ensure that our intent and impact are the same.

When using these messages, we must remember to do so repetitiously, logically and consistently. This requires that we provide the messages in a recurring manner in order to solidify the lessons and increase the likelihood that they will adopt the principles as their own. It also requires us to remain mindful of situations that connect soundly to the lessons that we are teaching. We can't expect our children to adopt these messages after hearing it only once. Therefore, intentional and repetitive use of the messages, accompanied by engaging discussion, is the optimal approach to utilizing this strategy.

We recognize that our messages have taken root in our child when they use them themselves. They may share the messages with their friends and teachers, or they may use our messages on us. They may simply apologize, forgive, or thank. Or, they may encourage us to believe in ourselves, when we struggle to do so on our own. They may remind us to own our behaviors, when we do something that requires us to take responsibility. And, they may profess to love us no matter what, when we need it the most. Yes, they will return the favor and provide for us the gifts we need, when we need it, just as we do for them. And, surprisingly, they do so at a very young age. Regardless of what they choose to replicate, we will undoubtedly feel pride in our ability to provide our children with tangible tools that spread love, confidence, happiness, integrity, and resilience with us and the world around them.

In closing, as parents, we use intentional messaging to provide our children with a clear plan for how to live their lives. Until our children adopt these messages as their own, we provide for them our love, confidence, happiness, integrity and resilience. We love them until they love themselves; we believe in them until they believe in themselves; we encourage happiness until they choose it themselves; we expect integrity until they expect it of themselves; and we help them to navigate life until they can brave life on their own.

Quick Guide: Intentional Messages Synopsis

Intentional Message	Targeted Concept	Outcome Pillar
I love you no matter what!	Unconditional Love	Love
I'm giving you my love, do you feel it?	Comfort	
I'm always with you, in your heart and in your thoughts.	Reassurance	
I love that you are a part of this family.	Belonging	
I believe in you, now believe in yourself.	Self-Belief	Confidence
You can do this.	Self-Efficacy	
Be the best you that you can be!	Self-Image	
Sing loud and proud.	Self-Pride	

How does that make you feel? How do you think they feel?	Awareness	Happiness
Choose to be happy.	Positivity	
Kindness.	Kindness	
Quick to apologize. Quick to forgive.	Forgiveness	
You are not bad; you made a bad choice.	Decision Making	Integrity
Always tell me the truth.	Honesty	
If you're brave enough to do it, be brave enough to own it!	Accountability	
It's your responsibility to stay close to me.	Responsibility	
You aren't supposed to know. That's why we learn.	Lifelong Learning	Resilience
There's always a solution.	Problem Solving	
Don't give up!	Persistence	
Thank you!	Gratitude	

Quick Guide:
Parent Perspective

Love	
Unconditional Love	*I love you no matter what!*

When I tell my children that I love them no matter what, I hope they truly believe that my love is intense, powerful, meaningful, everlasting, and without any conditions on who they are now, who they will become, and how they behave. I want them to feel the care I have for them, understand that it is permanent, and know that they do not need to work to gain my love. My love is *free* and flowing for them. And, it always will be.

Comfort	*I'm giving you my love, do you feel it?*

I give my children big heart-to-heart hugs and tell them I'm giving you my love, do you feel it when I know they are struggling with a situation. I use this message because I want them to know that I care about what they are experiencing, I'm here to help them get through it, and I support them in their process. My hope is that they let me share in their experiences so that I can help them learn to manage their feelings. I want them to know that they are not alone in facing their fears and they can depend on me to support them through life.

Reassurance	*I'm always with you, in your heart and in your thoughts.*

I tell my children that I'm always with you, in your heart and in your thoughts to give them the extra support, comfort and reassurance that although we may be apart, they can call upon my love by thinking of me. I want them to be able to control their own fears and doubts by using the love in our relationship to make them feel secure and happy. And, I want them to know that although I may not be in their presence physically, my love is permanent and with them always.

Belonging	*I love that you are a part of this family.*

I tell my children that I love that they are part of this family to reinforce my gratitude and love for them and to showcase that each and every member of our family is significant and valued as part of the entire system. I want to make a point to my children that no matter where they are in the world, they will always belong somewhere, specifically here, as part of this family. And, I hope that this encourages them to be active and positive participants in the other teams, organizations, groups, or systems they join throughout their lives.

Confidence

Self-Belief	*I believe in you, now believe in yourself.*

When I tell my children that I believe in you, now believe in yourself, my hope is that they take my belief in them and internalize it. I want them to use the message as encouragement to participate in something new, push through something challenging, and embrace the opportunities before them. I want them to truly believe that they are good people, using this to push through any negative thoughts and feelings. And, I want them to be secure in who they are and know that through failures they will learn and through learning they will grow and through growth they will be happy.

Self-Efficacy	*You can do this.*

I choose to use the message, you can do this, as a way to help my children push through their fears and uncertainties in life as they are exploring new situations, tackling challenging ones, or trying to improve their skills. Self-doubt is a terrible enemy of self-confidence. Learning, however, is its truest friend. Because I want my children to be confident in their beliefs about their capabilities through learning, I choose to encourage them through the trials and tribulations of childhood, until they learn to encourage themselves on their own.

Self-Image	*Be the best you that you can be!*

I want my children to understand that life is about learning and growing. We are never done exploring, shaping, tweaking, or honing our true beings. I want them to love themselves, accept themselves, understand who they are, dream of who they want to become, and work toward that goal, separate from me, in order to reach their fullest potential. I tell them to be the best you that you can be so that they become confident in who they are and embrace the concept of continuous growth.

Self-Pride	*Sing loud and proud.*

I use the message, sing loud and proud, as a way to ease the anxiety of performance situations in order for my children to have fun, embrace who they are, and feel confident participating in these types of situations. I believe that if I encourage pride in them, they will then enjoy accomplishments and develop good habits for approaching future tasks. This will lead to healthier, happier children who believe in themselves and take the risks associated with performance to feel the rewards of their accomplishments. I hope that they embrace who they are and show the world, free from fear and judgment.

Happiness

Awareness	*How does that make you feel?* *How do you think they feel?*

It is important to me for my children to label their feelings so that I can validate that their feelings are real and allowed. When we deny our feelings exist or act as if they are unimportant, we often end up feeling worse about ourselves. I do not want that for my children. I want to give them every opportunity to understand and control their emotions and feelings so that they accept their feelings as part of who they are. At the same time, I want them to develop a respect for others to become caring, compassionate people who value and show concern for others by helping them to recognize that others have feelings, too. I hope that my children acquire healthy concern and respect for themselves and others.

Positivity	*Choose to be happy.*

I remind my children to choose to be happy to help them develop positivity, optimism, resilience and problem solving skills. I hope that they choose to enjoy the experiences life offers by focusing on being happy so that they don't miss out. I also believe that children want to be in control. By telling them that they can choose happiness, they feel like they can control it and they are move likely to put it into practice. As a result, I've often noticed in negative situations, my children focus on the good instead of grating on the bad, which makes me believe that the foundation of happiness is present.

Kindness	*Kindness.*

Kindness is highly important to me because I believe it is the foundation for health and happiness. I'm particularly intentional in building kindness within my children due to the positive outcomes of social, personal and academic success associated with it. Additionally, I believe that by teaching them to embrace kindness, they will not only be kind to others but they will also develop kindness toward themselves. In my opinion, in an ever-changing world that dishes out negativity, they will need to rely on their self-worth and self-love to get them through. I think kindness is the key. My hope is that through a kindness-mindset, my children will have less anxiety and more self-love.

Forgiveness	*Quick to apologize. Quick to forgive.*

Forgiveness is good for our wellbeing because it allows us to move past negative experiences to more positive ones. I want my children to own their mistakes and poor decisions by apologizing but it is equally important to me that they give others the grace of forgiveness when they are wronged as well. If we hope for people to learn from their mistakes and grow, we have to allow them to get past those poor choices by providing them with an opportunity to reconcile. It benefits everyone when we can move forward in a positive manner.

Integrity	
Decision Making	*You are not bad; you made a bad choice.*
I believe that if we want to create good people, then we set the expectation that our children are good. Therefore, when they make mistakes, these choices may be bad, but that does not mean that my child is bad. I, particularly want to protect their self-concept – how they view themselves. So, it is important to me to ensure that each choice does not lead them to feel like a bad person, but that each choice can be made better next time, resulting in better choices in the future while maintaining good children in the process.	
Honesty	*Always tell me the truth.*
I believe that trust is the basis for all good relationships. Honesty brings about trust. If I am honest with my children, they will in turn be honest with me. If I expect honesty from them, they will learn to be honest. While pure honesty is not always socially acceptable, teaching my children how to be honest in a polite, respectful manner will give them a foundation for understanding how to deliver truthful messages in a kind way. In the end, I want my children to be honest so that they feel good about themselves and so that we can trust one another. In the end, I believe this will positively contribute to their morals and integrity.	
Accountability	*If you're brave enough to do it, be brave enough to own it!*
I believe that there is an overall lack of ownership over the negative actions and words we put out into the world these days. As a parent who values kindness and positivity, I want my children to think before they act and to spread love not hate. To that end, I believe that if more people were held accountable for their actions or the things they say, they would stop the negative behavior. So, I teach my children that if we are brave enough to engage in a behavior, we need to own it; take responsibility; show our flaws. This helps to build their honesty and responsibility, as I hold them accountable for their actions. Hopefully, this will also help shape them toward a positive persona as they avoid making poor choices.	

Responsibility	*It's your responsibility to stay close to me.*
I want to build responsibility early on in my children to help them gain some independence and feel a sense of control over their lives. Therefore, I chose to do so with their safety. By teaching them ways to protect themselves in their environment and their responsibility to stay close to me, I believe they learn that they play a role in their safety in order to learn to make choices to protect themselves from the dangers of the world. It starts with the dangers associated with moving cars and strangers in the grocery store, but the lessons broaden to other areas of their lives as they age.	

Resilience

Lifelong Learning	*You aren't supposed to know. That's why we learn.*
Learning is an important emphasis in parenting my children. I want them to view life as an opportunity to grow and develop continuously. Through a love of learning and a commitment to learning over a lifetime, their opportunities are endless. They can accomplish whatever they want to as long as they understand that through effort and commitment they can learn anything. Additionally, lifelong learning alleviates the pressures of perfectionism and encourages self-reflection, both of which I view as helpful for persisting through life, regardless of the challenges they may face. In short, I view lifelong learning as the impetus for my children's success.	

Problem Solving	*There's always a solution.*
I'm always happily impressed when my children voluntarily offer solutions to problems or present options for addressing an issue. I want them to consider consequences of their choices. I know they will make mistakes, they will get frustrated, maybe even angry, but because they know how to come up with solutions, they will be at an advantage later in life. I want to set them up to function independently and know that regardless of the situation, there is always a solution. I believe that this will allow them to look at life more positively and feel more in control of their lives, resulting in them being more resilient.	

Persistence	*Don't give up!*

It is important that my children understand that life is not always easy, even when we make good decisions. The most rewarding things in life are difficult to attain, which makes them even more meaningful. I want my children to realize their goals and dreams by putting forth the effort, time, and practice. They must stay in the struggle in order to attain their goals. I believe that my respectful encouragement is helpful as a motivator until they figure out how to self-motivate to persist without me.

Gratitude	*Thank you!*

Gratitude is a simple jester with complex, robust benefits. It encourages mindfulness, self-reflection, awareness, positivity, kindness, and virtue – all lessons that I want my children to embrace – in one act. It also comes with the added benefits of contributing to my child's resilience and success, providing lasting positive outcomes. Therefore, I encourage my children to practice gratitude so that they are courteous, thoughtful people who view others with equal respect and kindness.

Quick Guide:
Child Perspective

Love	
Unconditional Love	*I love you no matter what!*
I feel happy. It means a lot to me because it means you know me really good and you love me even if I do bad things. No matter what I do, no matter where I am, you love me.	
Comfort	*I'm giving you my love, do you feel it?*
It means that you are helping me not be scared or afraid because you are by my side. And, it makes me feel loved and happy. I feel it.	
Reassurance	*I'm always with you, in your heart and in your thoughts.*
It really does help me because I feel you in my heart, I feel like I'm always loved, and I know that at the end of the day, I will see you again.	
Belonging	*I love that you are a part of this family.*
It makes me feel happy because I'm part of this family and I know that everybody in this family loves me.	
Confidence	
Self-Belief	*I believe in you, now believe in yourself.*
It makes me feel like you believe in me, are always by my side, that I can do anything, and that I can trust in myself.	

Self-Efficacy	*You can do this.*
It makes me feel confident. If I'm scared to do something, it makes me feel less scared. And, if I think I can, I really can do it.	

Self-Image	*Be the best you that you can be!*
I believe it means to be the best you that you can be. The best me is kind, funny, and loves my family and friends.	

Self-Pride	*Sing loud and proud.*
This means that I will sing loud so everyone can hear me and I will be happy, too.	

Happiness	
Awareness	*How does that make you feel?*
It means that you want to know what I'm feeling and why. It helps me to be able to tell you my feelings.	

Awareness	*How do you think they feel?*
It helps me to see how other people feel so I can try helping them or say sorry to make them feel better if I did something wrong.	

Positivity	*Choose to be happy.*
It makes me feel generous and strong and it helps me be happy because I feel like I can choose to be happy.	

Kindness	*Kindness.*
It reminds me to be kind to others, whether they are family, friends, or even other people.	

Forgiveness	*Quick to apologize. Quick to forgive.*

This makes me feel better because I know that I can apologize and will be forgiven. When you forgive me, I feel loved because even if you are disappointed, you forgive me. It is important to me when you apologize because you are saying you are sorry and that others make mistakes, too. I forgive you because I know that you always forgive me, too.

Integrity

Decision Making	*You are not bad; you made a bad choice.*

It means that even though I know I made a bad choice or did something wrong, I'm not a bad person.

Honesty	*Always tell me the truth.*

It reminds me to always tell the truth and never lie because you won't trust me anymore.

Accountability	*If you're brave enough to do it, be brave enough to own it!*

If I'm not brave enough to tell you about it, I probably shouldn't do it. I think twice about doing bad things because I don't want to have to own it.

Responsibility	*It's your responsibility to stay close to me.*

It means that you are trying to keep me safe by teaching me how to protect myself.

Resilience

Lifelong Learning	*You aren't supposed to know. That's why we learn.*

It means to me that even though I want to get things right on my first try, I don't have to because I am just learning it. There are things that I shouldn't know yet. It also reminds me that I need to learn more.

Problem Solving	*There's always a solution.*
It means that there is more than one solution to a problem, if you just keep trying you will be able to figure it out on your own. If not, I can always ask for help but there is always a way to work things out.	

Persistence	*Don't give up!*
It means that I should try until I get something even though it is hard. It makes me feel like you are encouraging me to keep going. And, when I hear it, I don't want to give up. I want to keep going.	

Gratitude	*Thank you!*
It makes me feel happy when you tell me thank you. Saying thank you means you are respecting people and has good consequences, like when I waived at the lady that let us cross the road; she waived back.	

204

Create Your Own:
Ten Tips

10 Tips to Create and Use Intentional Messages

Tip #1: Identify.
- ➤ Determine the lessons you want to teach your child.
- ➤ Identify your child's deficiencies that you want to improve.
- ➤ Pinpoint behaviors you want to correct in your child.

Tip #2: Choose (carefully).
- ➤ Avoid confusing words or words with negative connotations.
- ➤ Select words that promote positivity and clearly connect to the lesson.
- ➤ Construct it in an imperative statement or question.

Tip #3: Simplify.
- ➤ Use clear, concrete, simple words.
- ➤ Choose words that you will easily remember.
- ➤ Choose words that your child will easily understand.

Tip #4: Express.
- ➤ Select messages that reflect who you are as a parent.
- ➤ Use messages that you can model through your own behavior.
- ➤ Develop messages that reflect the needs of you, your child, and your family.
- ➤ Use reflection to ensure that the message:
  - Is relevant for your children.
  - Helps to build your parent-child relationship.
  - Reflects a message that you want your children to understand and believe.
  - Helps to encourage your children to be happy.
  - Helps to alleviate your children's feelings of anxiety or sadness.

Tip #5: Try.
- ➤ Use it and observe how your child responds.
- ➤ Determine your child's understanding of the message and the lesson.
- ➤ Check to be sure you are comfortable with saying it aloud.

Tip #6: Commit.
- ➤ Use it often when promoting a new behavior.
- ➤ Use it at every opportunity that corresponds to the lesson in order to change a behavior.

Tip #7: Reinforce.
- ➤ Anticipate that it takes time and many reminders to develop and solidify.
- ➤ Use it with other messages to reinforce multiple lessons at once.

Tip #8: Discuss.
Ask questions to understand your child and their behavior better.
> - Use facilitated dialogue to explain situations and outline expectations.
> - Encourage reflection so that your child can identify their feelings, thoughts, and behaviors as it applies to the lesson and/or given situation.

Tip #9: Assess.
> - Examine the connectedness of the message and the lesson.
> - Look for results through behavior and/or attitude changes.
> - Determine if your child is responding well to the prompts.

Tip #10: Adapt.
> - Change the message if it's not working after a hardy effort.
> - Tweak the message if you find a better alternative.
> - Advance it to meet the needs of your children as they age.
> - Move on if your child has mastered the lesson.

Create Your Own:
Selected Messages

For easy reference, include in the following table your personalized, intentional messages or those you selected from the book.

Love	
Unconditional Love	*I love you no matter what!*
My Message:	
Comfort	*I'm giving you my love, do you feel it?*
My Message:	
Reassurance	*I'm always with you, in your heart and in your thoughts.*
My Message:	

Belonging	*I love that you are a part of this family.*
My Message:	

Confidence	
Self-Belief	*I believe in you, now believe in yourself.*
My Message:	
Self-Efficacy	*You can do this.*
My Message:	
Self-Image	*Be the best you that you can be!*
My Message:	
Self-Pride	*Sing loud and proud.*
My Message:	

Happiness	
Awareness	*How does that make you feel?*
My Message:	
Awareness	*How do you think they feel?*
My Message:	
Positivity	*Choose to be happy.*
My Message:	
Kindness	*Kindness.*
My Message:	
Forgiveness	*Quick to apologize. Quick to forgive.*
My Message:	

Integrity	
Decision Making	*You are not bad; you made a bad choice.*
My Message:	
Honesty	*Always tell me the truth.*
My Message:	
Accountability	*If you're brave enough to do it, be brave enough to own it!*
My Message:	
Responsibility	*It's your responsibility to stay close to me.*
My Message:	

Resilience	
Lifelong Learning	*You aren't supposed to know. That's why we learn.*
My Message:	
Problem Solving	*There's always a solution.*
My Message:	
Persistence	*Don't give up!*
My Message:	
Gratitude	*Thank you!*
My Message:	

References

Aknin, L. B., Dunn, E. W., & Norton, M. I. (2012). Happiness runs in a circular motion: Evidence for a positive feedback loop between prosocial spending and happiness. *Journal of Happiness Studies, 13*(2), 347-355.

Bandura, A. (2006). Guide for constructing self-efficacy scales. *Self-efficacy beliefs of adolescents, 5*(1), 307-337.

Bauchner, H., Vinci, R., & May, A. (1994). Teaching parents how to comfort their children during common medical procedures. *Archives of disease in childhood, 70*(6), 548.

Bong, M. & Skaalvik, E. M. (2003). Academic self-concept and self-efficacy: How different are they really? *Educational psychology review, 15*(1), 1-40.

Brocato, M. B., Roche, L. R., & McGuire, S. Y. (2018). Metacognition: The foundation of the century learning center. *Learning Centers in the 21st Century: A Modern Guide for Learning Assistance Professionals in Higher Education.* Bentonville, AR: Iona Press.

Brown, P., Roediger, H. & McDaniel, M. (2014). *Make it stick.* Boston, MA: Harvard University.

Demirci, İ. & Ekşi, H. (2018). Keep calm and be happy: A mixed method study from character strengths to well-being. *Educational Sciences: Theory & Practice, 18*(2).

Duckworth, A. (2016). *Grit: The power of passion and perseverance* (Vol. 234). New York, NY: Scribner.

Dweck, C. (2006). *Mindset: The new psychology of success.* New York, NY: Random House.

Evrard, P. (retrieved 2/6/2019). 10 signs of truly confident people. Retrieved online from: https://www.lifehack.org/285774/10-signs-truly-confident-people.

Flook, L., Goldberg, S. B., Pinger, L., & Davidson, R. J. (2014). Promoting prosocial behavior and self-regulatory skills in preschool children through a mindfulness-based kindness curriculum. *Developmental psychology, 51*(1), 44–51.

Grenville-Cleave, B. (2012). *Positive Psychology*. New York, NY: MJF Books.

Heyler, S. G., Armenakis, A. A., Walker, A. G., & Collier, D. Y. (2016). A qualitative study investigating the ethical decision making process: A proposed model. *The Leadership Quarterly, 27*(5), 788-801.

Kleitman, S. & Moscrop, T. (2010). Self-confidence and academic achievements in primary-school children: Their relationships and links to parental bonds, intelligence, age, and gender. In Trends and prospects in metacognition research (pp. 293-326). Springer, Boston, MA.

Maslow, A. H. (1943). A theory of human motivation. *Psychological Review, 50*(4), 370.

McGuire, S. Y. (2015). *Teach students how to learn: Strategies you can incorporate into any course to improve student metacognition, study skills, and motivation*. Stylus Publishing, LLC.

Morin, A. (retrieved 5/8/2020). How to teach kids problem solving skills. Retrieved online from: https://www.verywellfamily.com/teach-kids-problem-solving-skills-1095015.

Oxford Living Dictionaries. (2018). Retrieved online from: https://en.oxforddictionaries.com/.

Pajares, F. & Schunk, D. H. (2002). Self and self-belief in psychology and education: A historical perspective. In *Improving academic achievement* (pp. 3-21). Academic Press.

Park, N. & Peterson, C. (2006). Character strengths and happiness among young children: Content analysis of parental descriptions. *Journal of Happiness Studies, 7*(3), 323-341.

Rana, S., Hariharan, M., Nandinee, D., & Vincent, K. (2014). Forgiveness: A determinant of adolescents' happiness. *Indian Journal of Health and Wellbeing, 5*(9), 1119-1123.

Top Tier Leadership (retrieved 2/6/2019). Power of confidence: 7 characteristics of a confidence person. Retrieved online from: http://www.toptierleadership.com/blog/power-of-confidence-7-characteristics-of-a-confident-person/.

Tracy, J. L. & Robins, R. W. (2007). Emerging insights into the nature and function of pride. *Current directions in psychological science, 16*(3), 147-150.

Welwood, J. (1985). On love: Conditional and unconditional. *Journal of Transpersonal Psychology, 17*(1), 33-40.

Wilson, J. T. (2016). Brightening the Mind: The Impact of Practicing Gratitude on Focus and Resilience in Learning. *Journal of the Scholarship of Teaching and Learning, 16*(4), 1-13.

Glossary

G

gratitude: being thankful or showing appreciation
grit: resolve

H

happiness: the state of being happy
happy: feeling or showing pleasure or contentment
honest: sincere; free of deceit
honesty: quality of being honest

I

impact: the resulted effect of an action
intent: the anticipated effect of an action
intentional: deliberate; done with purpose
intrinsic: internal

J

innate: inborn; natural
integrity: the quality of being honest and having strong moral principles

K

kindness: showing care and concern for others

L

lifelong learning: an ongoing process of acquiring new knowledge and skills
love: an intense feeling of deep affection

M

metaemotion: ability to identify and regulate emotions and feelings
mindful: conscious or aware

mindfulness: the practice of intense focus in order to become conscious or aware
mindset: one's established set of attitudes

N

negativity: the practice of being negative or pessimistic in attitude
negativity bias: giving more weight and focus to negative experiences, emotions, and information

O

optimism: hopefulness regarding the future or situational outcomes
ownership: the act of acknowledging one's actions

P

parental love: a deep affection for our children
persistence: continued engagement in a course of action in spite of difficulty or opposition
positivity: the practice of being positive or optimistic in attitude
problem solving: the practice of fixing difficult situations or complex tasks

R

reassurance: removing doubts or fears
reconciliation: the restoration of friendly relations
reflection: the act of giving serious thought or consideration
resilience: ability to bounce back from setbacks; toughness
responsibility: the opportunity to make decisions independently

S

self-awareness: conscious knowledge of oneself
self-belief: accepted truths about oneself

self-concept: the ideas one constructs about themselves based off of the response of others
self-confidence: belief in one's abilities or qualities
self-efficacy: belief in one's capabilities to complete tasks
self-esteem: belief in one's qualities or worth
self-image: the idea of one's appearance
self-pride: a sense of pleasure or satisfaction in oneself
self-talk: internal dialogue; the messages one tells oneself

U
unconditional love: love free from conditions or limits

Index

About the Author

Lahna Rung Roche is a licensed professional counselor, learning specialist, and educator with twenty years of experience working with educational organizations to enhance student learning and success. With degrees in psychology and mental health counseling, Lahna, a lifelong LSU Tiger, has spent her life concentrating on her passion – learning. She supplements her passion for learning by gaining knowledge herself or by advancing learning for others. She values relationships above all else and believes her life's purpose is to help others be the best versions of themselves. Being a parent is the greatest surprise and treasure of Lahna's life. She resides in south Louisiana with her family – her husband, two children, and four pets.